Volume 28    Number 2    1999

# Discourse Processes

A MULTIDISCIPLINARY JOURNAL

**Special Issue:
Empirical Studies of Literature:
Selected Papers From IGEL '98
Guest Editor:
David S. Miall**

## Contents

Editor's Introduction . . . . . . . . . . . . . . . . . . . . . . . . . . . . 107
   *David S. Miall*

Genres of Discourse and the Definition of Literature. . . . . . . . . . . . . . . . . . 109
   *Gerard Steen*

What Is Literariness? Three Components of Literary Reading . . . . . . . . . . . . . 121
   *David S. Miall and Don Kuiken*

Metaphorical (In)Coherence in Discourse . . . . . . . . . . . . . . . . . . . . . 139
   *Yeshayahu Shen and Noga Balaban*

Readers as Text Processors and Performers:
A New Formula for Poetic Intonation. . . . . . . . . . . . . . . . . . . . . . . 155
   *Tom Barney*

Spotlight on Spectators: Emotions in the Theater . . . . . . . . . . . . . . . . . 169
   *Elly A. Konijn*

# EDITOR'S INTRODUCTION

The sixth conference of the International Society for the Empirical Study of Literature, or IGEL, was held August 1998 in Utrecht, Holland, hosted by the University of Utrecht and directed by Els Andringa. Previous conferences have been held at Siegen (1987), Amsterdam (1990), Memphis, Tennessee (1992), Budapest (1994), and Nakoda Lodge, near Banff, Canada (1996). The conferences bring together a wide range of scholars concerned with understanding the place and role of literature in its social, historical, psychological, linguistic, and other dimensions and who seek to advance our knowledge through empirical methods or more effective theoretical perspectives that may lead to empirical research.

This selection is based on articles from the 1998 conference and represents just a small part of its rich variety. Articles were solicited for this special issue and were subjected to the usual peer review process prior to publication. The issue opens with two articles that, from rather different perspectives, seek to refine our understanding of what is literary: Steen's article proposes that the literary domain requires definition within an improved theory of discourse genres; the article by Miall and Kuiken, in contrast, seeks to identify a set of response processes that are said to be characteristic of literary interaction. We then offer three articles that focus on specific research issues. Shen and Balaban argue that the coherence said to be provided by the root metaphors of discourse, according to the conceptual metaphor view, is not apparent in their sampling of evidence. Barney, a specialist in the sound structures of poetry, advances a new formula for identifying what is distinctive in the patterns of spoken verse. Finally, Konijn reports a study that assesses the motives and responses of audiences of theater performances, focusing in particular on the nature and object of their emotions. Other articles from the conference appear in parallel special issues of *Spiel* and *Poetics*.

The seventh biannual IGEL conference will be held at Victoria College, University of Toronto, July 31 to August 4, 2000. Topics include reading processes, literary institutions, media and literature, historical reception, literary creation, social and cultural contexts, as well as media and advertising. Please address inquiries to Gerald C. Cupchik (cupchik@scar.utoronto.ca), IGEL President, University of Toronto at Scarborough, 1265 Military Trail, Scarborough, Ontario,

Correspondence and requests for reprints should be sent to David S. Miall, Department of English, University of Alberta, Edmonton, Alberta, Canada T6G 2E5. E-mail: David.Miall@ualberta.ca

Canada M1C 1A4. Phone: 416–287–7467. Fax: 416–287–7642. Conference Web Site: http://citd.scar.utoronto.ca/igel2000/index.html.

For further information on the sixth IGEL conference (August 1998) and other activities, see the IGEL Web site at: http://www.lumis.uni-siegen.de/igel/

*David S. Miall*
Guest Editor

# Genres of Discourse
# and the Definition of Literature

### Gerard Steen
*Department of Discourse Studies*
*Tilburg University*
*Tilburg, The Netherlands*

There is a direct relation between genres of discourse and the definition of literature. A prototype–theoretical perspective on the classification of discourse can reveal that such genres as the novel, the poem, and the play, as well as such superordinate classes of discourse as literature, advertising, and academic writing, are all distinct classes of discourse but at different levels of abstraction. More important, superordinate, basic level, and subordinate classes of discourse have different numbers of typical values for the range of possible discourse attributes. The question of the definition of literature is, hence, related to the literary genres from which literature is abstracted, although the study of literary genres and literature is also connected to the study of nonliterary genres and other discourse classes. Such an approach can also explain what goes wrong in some recent proposals on the definition of literary discourse.

What kind of discourse is literature? What sort of theoretical category should be reserved for literary discourse in a general taxonomy of discourse? Is it a function, as has been proposed by Brewer (1995)? Is it a domain, as has been suggested by Schmidt (1982)? Or is the issue more complex than that, as argued in this article?

It is the aim of this contribution to address these questions. To provide an answer to the question of the definition of literature, it is first necessary to develop a general approach to the classification of discourse. The next section discusses the nature of literature within this general framework. The descriptive and explanatory potential of this approach is finally suggested in the conclusion.

## TOWARD A TAXONOMY OF DISCOURSE

It is an astonishing fact that discourse psychologists have not been overly concerned with creating a sophisticated taxonomy of discourse. With an explicit reference to work done on literary comprehension, the need for such a taxonomy

---

Correspondence and requests for reprints should be sent to Gerard Steen, Department of Discourse Studies, Tilburg University, P.O. Box 90153, 5000 LE Tilburg, The Netherlands. E-mail: g.j.steen@kub.nl

was recently acknowledged by, for instance, Graesser, Gernsbacher, and Goldman (1997). However, their suggestion that we develop the traditional quartet of narrative, expository, persuasive, and descriptive discourse into a "more mature classification scheme [with] numerous subcategories, as well as hybrids" (p. 315) is still too simple and monodimensional to capture the complexities of relations between all kinds of discourse.

The work on literature referred to by Graesser et al. (1997) has been carried out by literary scholars who have undertaken empirical studies to examine the behavioral side of their subject, systematically opposing literary to nonliterary discourse as an experimental factor in their designs (e.g., Sanders & Redeker, 1993; Steen, 1994; Zwaan, 1993). However, the opposition between literary and nonliterary discourse is still a crude one, and its operationalization by means of popular genres such as short stories and poems on the one hand and news reports on the other raises all kinds of questions about the relations between genres and other groupings of classes of discourse, such as literature. This may have been the reason for a surge of interest in the notion of genre in what has come to be known as the empirical study of literature (e.g., Brewer, 1995; Fishelov, 1995; Viehoff, 1995). It is interesting to see that these theoretical contributions go back to both more traditional literary theoretical sources, such as Todorov (1976), Fowler (1982), and Bakhtin (1986), as well as to linguistic approaches to discourse, including Hymes (1972), Swales (1990), and Biber (1994).

The function of a general taxonomy of discourse is manifold. It may serve a linguistic purpose in the systematic ordering of text and talk into well-motivated categories of discourse in order to facilitate research into relations between linguistic features and discourse types (e.g., Biber, 1989). A discourse taxonomy may also have a psychological purpose, in that it provides a framework for the study of particular aspects of production and comprehension processes, such as the incidence of particular kinds of inferencing in narrative comprehension (e.g., Graesser & Kreuz, 1993). Finally, a taxonomy for discourse can also serve sociological ends, with respect to the delineation of particular large-scale social and cultural spheres of communication, variously called *domains, systems,* or *fields,* such as the one of science (e.g., Berkenkotter & Huckin, 1995). Although the references suggest that work is being done in each of these areas today, categories, dimensions, and levels of abstraction vary between disciplines and domains of research, and a unified theoretical framework to a typology of discourse could help to align such projects.

It is clear that each of these functions is also relevant to the empirical study of literature. We need a systematic framework for the description and explanation of a particular body of discourse (e.g., van Peer, 1991), for the investigation of psychological processing issues related to that collection (e.g., Schram & Steen, 1992), and for the study of the macrosocial processes of interaction related to this body of discourse between groups of people inside and outside of institutions (e.g., Griswold, 1996). An approach to literary discourse genres that is not limited to literature would be useful in increasing the theoretical and empirical appeal of the results of empirical studies of literature.

The criterion for developing such a taxonomy should be a pragmatic or behavioral one: What we are interested in is how literary and nonliterary discourse are used by discourse participants in their various possible roles. This means that we need an individual's perspective on the classification of discourse, for it is the individual who engages the linguistic object as a product or stimulus of a particular kind, it is the individual who performs the mental processes of production and comprehension in relation to the discourse as a particular kind, and it is the individual who thereby participates in the more encompassing social processes of communicative interaction by means of the particular type of discourse in question. This assumption motivates adopting a cognitive psychological approach to discourse classification in the form of prototypical categorization theory (e.g., Paltridge, 1995).

Whether classes of discourse are regarded as natural or social kinds, they cannot be regarded as so-called definitional concepts, which permit description by means of necessary and sufficient conditions. Instead, it is plausible to assume that they are cognitively represented by means of prototypes. As is well known, a prototype is the most typical instance of a more encompassing and varied, fuzzy conceptual category. An example would be an apple as the prototype of a fruit. Such categories themselves can be ordered into three-tiered hierarchies of basic level concepts, subordinates, and superordinates (*apples, Golden Delicious,* and *fruit,* respectively). The basic level concepts embody the information level at which concepts are most easily recognized, remembered, and learned; the difference between alternative concepts is largest at this level of abstraction, whereas subordinate and superordinate concepts are less richly differentiated from their respective alternatives (e.g., the subordinates *Golden Delicious* vs. *Granny Smith*). Although the fuzzy and hierarchical aspects of prototypes may be seen as independent of each other, it is their combination that is essential for the development of this proposal (cf. Smith, 1988).

It should be noted that basic level prototypicality is affected by expertise, suggesting that the organization of resemblances and differences between categories is related to their function in use. Before we apply these notions to the development of a taxonomy of discourse, we should hence be explicit about our target of research: A generally valid taxonomy of discourse should not project our expert scientific view of discourse types onto the range of discourse but instead begin with an examination of discourse concepts as they are valid for ordinary language users. It is true that there may be a great degree of social and cultural variability in such knowledge, and some may feel this constitutes a threat to the very notion of literature itself. However, this only means that we just have to be more careful and specific in our use of genre concepts and related notions such as literature. It is an empirical question whether socially and culturally distinct concepts of discourse have sufficient overlap to be useful across cultural and linguistic communities. Apart from that, texts, including literary texts, are received and produced by concrete individuals with specific knowledge bases that need to be described (and, hopefully, explained). What is lacking for such an enterprise is a sufficiently sophisticated approach to the many complexities of discourse. It is the purpose of this article to make a very modest beginning with filling that theoretical gap; the empirical research that is needed to investigate these ideas may be illustrated by Fishelov (1995, 1998).

Given these assumptions, it is presumably the level of genre that embodies the basic level concepts, whereas subgenres are the conceptual subordinates, and more abstract classes of discourse are the superordinates. Thus, the genre of an advertisement is to be contrasted with that of a sermon, a recipe, a poem, and so on. These genres differ from each other on a whole range of attributes, to which we will return in a moment. The subordinates of the genre of the advertisement are less distinct from each other. The press advertisement, the radio commercial, the television commercial, the Internet advertisement, and so on, are mainly distinguished by one feature: their medium. The superordinate of the genre of the ad, advertising, is also systematically distinct from the other superordinates by means of only one principal attribute, the one of domain: It is "business" for advertising, but it exhibits the respective values of "religious," "domestic," and "artistic" for the other examples. There is an intuitive attraction, then, in adopting the prototype categorization framework as a starting point for the development of a more precise taxonomy of discourse.

This is especially so because fuzzy categories may be characterized by a number of attributes exhibiting different values. Thus, *fruit, apples,* and *Golden Delicious* are all characterized by their values regarding color, shape, size, taste, texture, and juiciness. The same holds true for classes of discourse at various levels of abstraction: They have values for at least the attributes of domain, medium, content, form, function, type, and language. Paltridge (1995) has a comparable list. Thus, an advertisement may be characterized as follows: Its domain is the one of business communication. Its medium may vary between written, spoken, and multimodal but typically involves a monologic discourse directed at a large and anonymous, if often well-specified, audience. Its content is almost free, except that it has to have a positive connotation. The form of an advertisement is extremely free; its function is to persuade the consumer that the product or service is good and often to exhort the consumer to go and get it. The discourse type of an advertisement may be either narrative or argumentative, descriptive or expository—each of these types seems equally possible. Its language is an odd mixture of formal and colloquial, usually fairly rhetorically structured, and includes professional register depending on the good advertised (cf. Cook, 1992).

It has to be emphasized here that this is a provisional characterization of a fuzzy category. It is possible to argue about almost all of the features listed previously, even though some seem to be more secure than others. It is certainly true that many advertisements do not exhibit all of the aforementioned characteristics.

For instance, as one reviewer pointed out to me, there are negative attack ads, particularly in political campaigns. However, that is precisely the advantage of adopting a prototypical approach to genre classification: It allows for fuzziness within a multidimensional discourse space. Moreover, the provisional characterization can be tested and corrected, both against informants' judgments about genre concepts as well as against informants' ratings of sets of texts.

This list of attributes may not be complete, but it captures a good deal of the variation between classes of discourse that has been examined in various disciplines contributing to discourse studies. Space forbids ample reference to research performed in each of these areas, but more general descriptions may perhaps suffice to indicate the kinds of work that can be invoked here. The easiest attribute is the one of language, in which stylistics, rhetoric, and sociolinguistics have traditionally been concerned with the study of diverging patterns of selection and combination of language items. Types of discourse are the major classes of narrative, argumentation, description, and exposition recognized of old, some of which have received extensive treatment in disciplines of their own (narratology and argumentation theory), whereas another subset, exposition, has become of increasing interest to discourse psychologists. Functions of discourse include central phenomena such as informative, persuasive, and instructive intentions, which have been studied in cognitive and social psychology and education. By forms of discourse are meant generic superstructures in the sense of van Dijk (1995; for the news report, the scientific article, and so on), but there are also more generally used text patterns such as the problem–solution structure—rhetoreticians have traditionally had a large stake in this field. Contents of discourse refers to more or less controversial topics and themes studied in, for instance, critical approaches to discourse, such as gender, class, race, ethnicity, and so on. The medium of discourse involves linguistic and nonlinguistic aspects of the material means by which a message is transmitted, and it has been studied by linguists, semioticians, and mass media scholars. Finally, domains of discourse involve the concept of large-scale social and cultural organizations of reality into spheres of communication with rules, norms, and conventions of their own, such as art, science, religion, business, politics, government, and so on; this aspect of discourse has been predominantly investigated by sociologists of language, mass communication, and culture. All of these aspects have been studied both within and between genres as they have been conceived previously, testifying to their applicability as attributes of discourse at various levels of abstraction (e.g., van Dijk, 1997).

This is a tantalizing sketch that raises more questions than it can answer at the moment. For instance, there is the matter of the number and nature of the attributes and their values. Moreover, some attributes have more variables—should they be seen as distinct attributes themselves? Another question involves the interrelations between the attributes. Then there is the problem of deciding which class of discourse is to be taken as a genre and which is not. These are just three issues that are on the agenda for further research into a taxonomy of discourse.

For now, we have to leave the general approach for what it is and attempt to show how it can be profitably used for the definition of literature.

## THE DEFINITION OF LITERATURE

There is a major advantage in adopting a prototypical categorization approach to the classification of discourse in connection with the empirical study of literature. This is the highlighting of the conceptual connection between distinct genres on the one hand and literature and its definition on the other. Following the approach outlined previously, literature may be argued to be the superordinate of genres such as the novel, the poem, and the play, each of which displays a number of familiar subgenres, such as the western, the detective, and so on, for the novel. It would follow that it might be harder to define the category of literature than the categories of novel, poem, or play, and this might accord with the experience of both ordinary language users as well as experts. An empirical study of literature that wishes to be in touch with other studies of discourse could do worse than explore the consequences of this ordering of the field. This is particularly useful because it redresses situations in which genre studies are pursued without much reference to the definition of literature, and vice versa.

Before we turn to such consequences, let us first examine some of the assumptions of this approach. The basic idea would be that the series of concepts *literature, novel,* and *western* is a hierarchy of concepts, of which the *novel* would be the basic level term, *literature* the superordinate, and *western* the subordinate. Language users would, hence, be predicted to have relatively richer representations of novels than of westerns or of literature, when these are compared to competing concepts at the same level, respectively, such as poems on the basic level, spy novels on the subordinate, and philosophy on the superordinate. To pursue this example somewhat further, a novel might be characterized as follows: Its content would be fictional and portray a significant action or process. Its form could be one of suspense, surprise, or curiosity (Brewer & Lichtenstein, 1982). Its type would be narrative in that semantically causal relations would somehow govern the text structure (e.g., van den Broek, 1994). Its function would be to positively affect the mood of the reader. Its medium would be printed matter for a mass readership. Its domain would be the one of the arts. Its language could be characterized, with Biber (1989), as "extremely narrative, moderately involved, situated, nonabstract, and not marked for persuasion" (p. 18). This is a rich and typical description of the concept of the novel, which should be easily recognizable to the ordinary language user. Again, however, it is probably wise to add a warning that we are talking about a prototype that may, moreover, be socially and culturally variable: As we have seen previously, such a caveat only suggests that there is a lot of empirical work to be done.

The novel may be fruitfully opposed to the poem. The content of a poem would also typically be fictional but would not be restricted to portraying a significant action or process. The form of a poem could be highly diverse, from the haiku and the epigram, through the sonnet and free verse, to the epic. Its type could be narrative but just as easily argumentative, descriptive, and expository. Its function would also be to positively affect the mood of the reader. Its medium could be printed matter for a mass readership, just like the novel, but oral poetry and poetry to music are just as common, so the medium does not seem to be fixed. Its domain would be the one of the arts, again, but its language should be characterized as relatively foregrounded in comparison with the novel (cf. Fishelov, 1998). In sum, function and domain would not be different between novel and poem, but form, type, medium, and language would be different. Content is both different and identical between the two in that fiction is an important shared characteristic.

This may lead to a description of the superordinate concept in these terms: Literature is a type of discourse that is characterized by the domain value "artistic," the content value "fictional," and the functional value "positively affective," or simply "divertive." Contrast this to the nature of the superordinate of *advertising* mentioned before, and it is clear that it, too, is mainly determined by the two attributes of domain and function, having the values of "business" and "persuasive," respectively; medium, form, type, and language are all unspecified for these two superordinates. In other words, the superordinates *literature* and *advertising* are positively distinguished from each other by means of two properties, whereas the basic level concepts *novel* and *poem* require five attributes for a correct discrimination between them. This is in support of the argument for the adoption of the prototype approach and its use of genres as basic level concepts.

One of the most striking and, at first glance, questionable features in this description of literature might be the one of "positively affective," or simply "divertive." Tragedy is a class of literature that seems in blatant contradiction with this value and raises the following question: How can it be accommodated? However, tragedy mainly has to do with the content of the literary text in that it deals with a negatively valenced story. It is one of the complex characteristics of literature that the reader may turn to sad stories to experience pleasure: The famous American critic Leslie Fiedler held that all literature is meant to water the emotions. In such cases, there is a clash between content and function that is typical of many texts belonging to this artistic domain. That negative mood triggered by negatively valenced content may be dominant during some stages of the reading process does not mean that the overall function of the text cannot be said to be divertive at the end of the day. According to Czech Structuralism, literature is typically characterized by experiencing pleasure in displeasure.

Let us turn to subordinate concepts. As has been pointed out by Brewer and Lichtenstein (1982), the thriller and the detective are kinds of novels that only differ from each other with respect to form, in that the causal structure of the events described is portrayed in a typically different order or form; in the terminology of prototypical categorization theory, they require only one attribute for their distinction. In poetry, elegies and odes exhibit no other constant difference than the one of content, which is positively or negatively valenced. A similar opposition may be observed between comedies and tragedies in plays. Hence, subordinates are also less richly differentiated from each other than are basic level concepts.

All of these comments are crude simplifications when it comes to examining individual instances of beautiful texts prized by the literary scholar, and many important aspects of literary comprehension have been omitted. But this is precisely why the theory of genres and the definition of literature have been problematic for so long. This proposal is not intended to be the answer to all of these problems; on the contrary, it is merely the beginning of a research program that requires a great deal of support from the expertise residing in traditional literary scholarship and its experience with individual texts. However, it also offers a framework for mobilizing and revealing that expertise in empirical work by pointing to the possibility of data collection on properties of classes of discourse in the manner of prototype categorization theory. That the definition of literature should be directly geared to people's experience of concrete genres and subgenres is a novel perspective on this issue, which may help explain why the category of literature itself is such an elusive category. This may not be due to the nature of literature itself but to the abstract nature of superordinates and our conceptualization of them as fuzzy categories. The approach, thus, ultimately aims to ground the distinctness of central literary genres and the specificity of the literary reading experience in the individual's conceptual repertoire, leaving ample scope for the role of representation by means of exemplars in a fashion that might be highly attractive to the traditional scholar. Moreover, the framework also guarantees that we link up with other instances of discourse processes outside literature, enhancing our understanding of constancies and variation between literary and nonliterary classes of discourse. To further strengthen the appeal of this proposal, let us finally take a brief look at some alternatives and explain what is wrong with them.

## SOME OTHER PROPOSALS

A prototypical approach emphasizes the hierarchical order of fuzzy concepts in a domain, using the same attributes for every level of conceptualization. From that perspective, there is a direct relation between genres of literary discourse and the definition of literature itself. They are all classes of discourse, with different numbers of typical values for the possible attributes at each level of abstraction. Let us examine how this starting point can explain the problems of some recent proposals.

Brewer (1995) advanced an interesting theoretical contribution on "Discourse Force and Empirical Studies of Literature." His concern was with the classification of genres, literary and nonliterary, according to "type of information" and "discourse force." The latter would be identical to our factor of function, whereas the former is a conflation of our factors of content and type. In addition to these factors, Brewer distinguished another factor, "text structure," which is our factor of "form." Brewer situated some 20-odd genres within his two-dimensional grid of Information Type × Discourse Force and points out some relations between particular combinations of values on the one hand and "text structures" on the other. There is a good number of details that would merit further discussion, but in this context, only one issue may receive extended treatment.

The dimension of discourse force has four values in Brewer's (1995) proposal: informative, entertaining, persuasive, and literary–aesthetic. If the basis of discourse force or function is the presumed effect of the text on the reader, "literary–aesthetic" is the odd one out: Texts can aim to entertain, inform, and persuade readers (and instruct, exhort, and direct them), but they cannot "literary–aesthetic" readers. They may have an aesthetic affect, but that is just one kind of affect, a specific form of "entertaining." The literary part of "literary–aesthetic" is either the same, or it is not a function but an indication of the domain of the text—that it is artistic. In that case, which is the interpretation I prefer, Brewer's taxonomy would require another dimension—the one of domain—which could have values such as "artistic," "scientific," "business," and so on. Treating literature as part of a domain of discourse is what sociologically oriented literary theorists have done for a while now, although few people would hazard to regard literature as a function.

As an aside, it should be noted that this does not mean that literature does not have a function, which, in some cases, may be to defamiliarize the reader's perceptions. Indeed, defamiliarization may be seen as one specific effect of the divertive discourse function, as was also suggested by the Czech Structuralists, and it can be traced by conducting empirical work of the kind referred to at the outset of this article. However, the point is that literature cannot be solely defined as a function, conceptualized as the expressive, divertive, informative, persuasive, and other presumed effects of a text on the reader. It is precisely the multidimensional nature of a prototypical approach to discourse genres that aims to accommodate the complex, multifaceted nature of literature, including features such as function and domain, besides some other ones.

The oddity of Brewer's (1995) proposal can be explained by connecting it to a taxonomy of more abstract classes of discourse, as is a natural thing to do in a prototype–theoretical approach. Just as genres such as poems and novels have values for attributes such as discourse force and so on, so do their superordinates, including literature. As a result, "literary" cannot come up as one value of the attribute of "discourse force" or "function" for the basic level concepts of the various concrete genres, for it is not a property of discourse but a superordinate category of discourse in itself. What we see happening in Brewer is the transformation of a superordinate concept (*literature*) into a value (*literary*) of an attribute (*function*) for the basic level categories (*concrete genres*). A more comprehensive prototypical approach with its emphasis on hierarchical ordering next to prototypical ordering highlights the need for the inclusion of literature as a defined, more abstract class of discourse.

If Brewer (1995) exemplified what happens when genres are discussed without due attention being paid to superordinates, the reverse may be observed in some of the work by the sociological approach to literature referred to just now. Such approaches sometimes deal with literature as a superordinate class of discourse without having sufficient recourse to the basic level terms of concrete genres out of which the superordinate arises. Literature is often regarded as a cultural domain governed by a set of conventions for social action, perhaps in connection with the typical function of achieving some kind of positive affect (Schmidt, 1982; cf. van Peer, 1991). This is an abstract definition of literature that is not very rich in itself, as is to be expected at the level of superordinates. What should not be forgotten, however, is the fact that such superordinates and their prototypical properties function in a larger conceptual system, in which it is the basic level terms that provide more meat to the entire domain. As we have seen, we know a lot about typical literary genres such as the poem and the novel, but the variation between them is too large to be uniformly reflected in the definition of their superordinate category, literature itself.

The problem in some of the more radical approaches to literature as a social domain, however, is that this basic level experience of literature is left aside. As a result, the impression may arise that concrete properties of texts with regard to language, medium, form, content, and type are immaterial when we speak about literature, leading to the conclusion that anything may be literature. To a certain extent this is true, but it also goes against our typical experience of literature through its basic level genres. The only explanation of this paradox is to adopt a prototypical and encompassing approach to the genres and definition of literature. It shows that almost any text as an instance of a specific genre may be dealt with as if it were literature, but it also shows that many such texts would be experienced as atypical examples of literature, which are far removed from what we would expect for the genre in question.

A final note may be in order about other superordinates, such as fiction and narrative. Fiction and narrative are two interesting and important superordinates that arise out of the grouping of texts according to values of attributes other than the one of domain. Fiction is one value of the attribute of content, whereas narrative is one value of the attribute of type. One observation that may be made is that some of these superordinates are more functional than others: Literature and its alternatives—academic writing, journalism, and so on—are probably more generally recognizable as superordinate classes of discourse than are fiction and narrative. Apparently, the domain factor is more important than the ones of content and type. Why is this? Moreover, fiction is beginning to be used as a functional label in bookshops, libraries, and review articles as well (Fishelov, 1995), but narrative is not. Why should this be? Yet Graesser and Kreuz (1993) used narrative as one of their four main factors in an inference generation model. Is this justifiable? It raises questions as to the weight of this particular superordinate in comparison with other conceivable ones, either derived from the same attribute (like argumentation), or from other attributes (like fiction for content, and so on). A prototypical approach to a taxonomy of discourse may be a good conceptual instrument to motivate the use of such abstract, superordinate categories of discourse in all kinds of studies, including studies of literary discourse.

## ACKNOWLEDGMENTS

This article was presented in an earlier form at the International Conference on the Empirical Study of Literature, Utrecht, The Netherlands, August 1998. I thank the audience for helpful comments and suggestions. I am also grateful to J. Lachlan Mackenzie, Wilbert Spooren, and Carel van Wijk for their comments on an earlier version of this article.

## REFERENCES

Bakhtin, M. M. (1986). *Speech genres and other late essays* (V. W. McGee, Trans., and C. Emerson & M. Holquist, Eds.). Austin: University of Texas Press.
Berkenkotter, C., & Huckin, T. N. (Eds.). (1995). *Genre knowledge in disciplinary communication: Cognition/culture/power.* Hillsdale, NJ: Lawrence Erlbaum Associates, Inc.
Biber, D. (1989). A typology of English texts. *Linguistics, 27,* 3–43.
Biber, D. (1994). An analytical framework for register studies. In D. Biber & E. Finegan (Eds.), *Sociolinguistic perspectives on register* (pp. 31–50). New York: Oxford University Press.
Brewer, W. F. (1995). Discourse force and empirical studies of literature. In G. Rusch (Ed.), *Empirical approaches to literature: Proceedings of the Fourth Biannual Conference of the International Society for the Empirical Study of Literature, IGEL* (pp. 89–95). Siegen, Germany: LUMIS-Publications.
Brewer, W. F., & Lichtenstein, E. H. (1982). Stories are to entertain: A structural-affect theory of stories. *Journal of Pragmatics, 6,* 473–486.
Cook, G. (1992). *The discourse of advertising.* London: Routledge.
Fishelov, D. (1995). Studying literary genres: The empirical angle. In G. Rusch (Ed.), *Empirical approaches to literature: Proceedings of the Fourth Biannual Conference of the International Society for the Empirical Study of Literature, IGEL* (pp. 84–88). Siegen, Germany: LUMIS-Publications.
Fishelov, D. (1998). The institutional definition of poetry: Some heretical thoughts. *Empirical Studies of the Arts, 16,* 5–13.
Fowler, A. (1982). *Kinds of literature.* Oxford, England: Oxford University Press.
Graesser, A. C., Gernsbacher, M. A., & Goldman, S. R. (1997). Cognition. In T. A. van Dijk (Ed.), *Discourse studies: A multidisciplinary introduction: Vol. 1. Discourse as structure and process* (pp. 292–319). London: Sage.
Graesser, A. C., & Kreuz, R. J. (1993). A theory of inference generation during text comprehension. *Discourse Processes, 16,* 145–160.
Griswold, W. (1996). Transformation of genre in Nigerian fiction: The case of the village novel. In R. J. Kreuz & M. S. MacNealy (Eds.), *Empirical approaches to literature and aesthetics* (pp. 573–582). Norwood, NJ: Ablex.
Hymes, D. (1972). Models of the interaction of language and social life. In J. Gumperz & D. Hymes (Eds.), *Directions in sociolinguistics: The ethnography of communication* (pp. 35–71). New York: Holt, Rinehart & Winston.
Paltridge, B. (1995). Working with genre: A pragmatic perspective. *Journal of Pragmatics, 24,* 393–406.
Sanders, J., & Redeker, G. (1993). Linguistic persective in short news stories. *Poetics, 22,* 69–87.

Schmidt, S. J. (1982). *Foundations for the empirical study of literature: The components of a basic theory.* Hamburg, Germany: Buske.

Schram, D. H., & Steen, G. J. (1992). "But what *is* literature?" A programmatic answer from the empirical study of literature. *SPIEL, 11,* 239–258.

Smith, E. E. (1988). Concepts and thought. In R. J. Sternberg & E. E. Smith (Eds.), *The psychology of human thought* (pp. 19–49). Cambridge, England: Cambridge University Press.

Steen, G. J. (1994). *Understanding metaphor in literature: An empirical approach.* London: Longman.

Swales, J. M. (1990). *Genre analysis: English in academic and research settings.* Cambridge, England: Cambridge University Press.

Todorov, T. (1976). The origin of genres. *New Literary History, 8,* 159–170.

van den Broek, P. (1994). Comprehension and memory of narrative texts: Inferences and coherence. In M. A. Gernsbacher (Ed.), *Handbook of psycholinguistics* (pp. 539–588). New York: Academic.

van Dijk, T. A. (1995). On macrostructures, mental models, and other inventions: A brief personal history of the Kintsch–van Dijk theory. In C. A. Weaver, III, S. Mannes, & C. R. Fletcher (Eds.), *Discourse comprehension: Essays in honor of Walter Kintsch* (pp. 383–410). Hillsdale, NJ: Lawrence Erlbaum Associates, Inc.

van Dijk, T. A. (Ed.). (1997). *Discourse studies: A multidisciplinary introduction.* London: Sage.

van Peer, W. (1991). But what *is* literature? Toward a descriptive definition of literature. In R. D. Sell (Ed.), *Literary pragmatics* (pp. 127–141). London: Routledge.

Viehoff, R. (1995). Literary genres as cognitive schemata. In G. Rusch (Ed.), *Empirical approaches to literature: Proceedings of the Fourth Biannual Conference of the International Society for the Empirical Study of Literature, IGEL* (pp. 72–76). Siegen, Germany: LUMIS-Publications.

Zwaan, R. A. (1993). *Aspects of literary comprehension.* Amsterdam: Benjamins.

# What Is Literariness?
# Three Components of Literary Reading

David S. Miall
*Department of English*
*University of Alberta*
*Edmonton, Canada*

Don Kuiken
*Department of Psychology*
*University of Alberta*
*Edmonton, Canada*

It is now widely maintained that the concept of *literariness* has been critically examined and found deficient. Prominent postmodern literary theorists have argued that there are no special characteristics that distinguish literature from other texts. Similarly, cognitive psychology has often subsumed literary understanding within a general theory of discourse processing. However, a review of empirical studies of literary readers reveals traces of literariness that appear irreducible to either of these explanatory frameworks. Our analysis of readers' responses to several literary texts (short stories and poems) indicates processes beyond the explanatory reach of current situation models. Such findings suggest a three-component model of literariness involving foregrounded stylistic or narrative features, readers' defamiliarizing responses to them, and the consequent modification of personal meanings.

What sort of activity is the reading of literature? There are several possible answers to this question, depending on the respondent's theoretical commitments. Reading literature may, for example, be understood as a type of discourse processing. That is, it may be a "second order effect," a particular organization of the cognitive processes that are also apparent in ordinary prose or conversation (Hobbs, 1990, p. 165). Or, reading literature may be the outcome of rhetorical devices designed to promote a particular ideology. In this view, "anything can be literature" or "can cease to be literature" depending on the prevailing doctrine (Eagleton, 1983, p. 10). Theories of both kinds, whether grounded in cognitive psychology or in postmodern theory, do not accord literary texts their distinctive-

---

Correspondence and requests for reprints should be sent to David S. Miall, Department of English, University of Alberta, Edmonton, Alberta, Canada T6G 2E5. E-mail: David.Miall@ualberta.ca

ness; both imply that any text, whether literary or not, depends on functions common to all texts. There purportedly are no processes unique to the act of literary reading (Miall & Kuiken, 1998).

In this article, we offer a challenge to these perspectives, focusing on our attempt to reconceptualize *literariness*. Unlike Jakobson, who first coined this term in 1921 (Erlich, 1981), we suggest that literariness cannot be defined simply as a characteristic set of text properties. On the other hand, neither can it be regarded as the result of applying a set of conventions (cf. Zwaan, 1993, pp. 7–15). We argue instead that literariness is the product of a distinctive mode of reading that is identifiable through three key components of response to literary texts. We describe several studies that provide evidence favoring this conception of literariness, evidence that appears difficult to understand either within the discourse processing or postmodern theoretical framework. We begin with one reader's account of a moment during reading that shows evidence of all three components of literariness.

In a recent empirical study, we invited 30 readers of two Coleridge poems to comment on the passages in these poems that they found striking. We focus on one participant's commentary (reported more fully by Sikora, Kuiken, & Miall, 1998) on the opening lines from "The Nightingale": "No cloud, no relique of the sunken day / Distinguishes the West . . ." (Coleridge, 1817/1924). The reader is explaining why she finds this passage striking:

> Because of the way that he says a "sunken day" and there is "no relique"; so there's nothing there. I like it because it's unusual to see the days sunken, instead of the sun. I think that's what gives it it's sense of desolation. I just picture this huge, huge expanse of sky with really nothing else on the horizon. There's also kind of a sense of timelessness; because relics are something that are old and sunken, it sounds like a sunken ship, something that's been there for hundreds of years and nobody knows about it, but it's something that's happening right now and it's kind of before dark but after day. It's just kind of a nothing time, well not a nothing time but a time that can't be described, that can't be categorized.

In these comments, we detect the three components of response that constitute literariness:

1. The reader initially comments on the style of the poem, "the way" it is written: "Because of the way that he says a 'sunken day' and there is 'no relique.'" The first component of literariness, as this reference suggests, is the occurrence of stylistic variations that are distinctively (although not uniquely) associated with literary texts: in this case, a metaphor (*sunken day*) and an archaic, polysemous noun (*relique*). (Later, we will broaden this component to include narrative features.)

2. The reader has been struck by these stylistic variations, remarking that "it's unusual to see the days sunken, instead of the sun." The more usual and familiar locution, the sunken sun, has been replaced by a phrase that unsettles the reader's conventional understanding of faded day. The second component of literariness is the occurrence of this type of defamiliarization.

3. The reader is prompted to reflect on the implications of this defamiliarizing phrase, implications that do not seem immediately obvious because several feelings and images are called to mind before a provisional judgment is reached. The phrase refers, she eventually concludes, to "a nothing time . . . a time that can't be described, that can't be categorized." In other words, the reader has been prompted to put in place a new sense of time, but her difficulty in finding the appropriate words attests to the reinterpretive effort required. Thus, the third component of literariness is the modification or transformation of a conventional feeling or concept.

The reader commentary we have just cited is unusual in exhibiting within a short space all three components of the phenomenon we have termed *literariness*. However, we suggest that all three must be present and must interact to constitute literariness. Briefly, literariness is constituted when stylistic or narrative variations defamiliarize conventionally understood referents and prompt reinterpretive transformations of a conventional feeling or concept. Each component of literariness (stylistic or narrative variations, defamiliarization, and reinterpretive transformations) may occur separately: Advertising copy, for example, often makes use of arresting stylistic features; traumatic events may precipitate the transformation of conventional feelings and concepts. We suggest however that the key to literariness is the interaction of these component processes. Rather than any special content, contextual conditions (e.g., educational practices), or ideological functions, literature is unique because it initiates a distinctive form of psychological change. This process of change is initiated under no other conditions that we are aware of, although comparable processes may be operative during response to some works of visual art, music, dance, or film.

The three components of literariness can be elaborated somewhat more technically in the following way. Literary texts contain features that stand out from ordinary language use—or are "foregrounded" (a term from Mukařovský, 1932/1964). In the example we cited, the poem deploys stylistic features within molecular noun phrases, but foregrounding may also be evident within molar narrative structures, through devices that provide shifts in point of view, contrasting thematic entities, or insights into character perspective through free, indirect discourse (these are just a few of the many devices that could be cited). Our proposal, in fact, is in accord with an extensive tradition of theorizing about literary stylistics from British Romantic writers such as Coleridge and Shelley, through the Russian Formalists, the Prague Linguistic Circle (of whom Mukařovský was a member), to more recent work by Leech, Fowler, Short, Widdowson, and others (reviewed by van Peer, 1986). At the narrative level, we can also refer to the work of Zholkovsky (1984), who has shown how entire themes can be transformed through contrast, augmentation, reduction, and other "expressive devices" to create a text's "poetic world" (p. 63).

Our approach entails specifying in detail, at the local textual level, what stylistic and narrative features prompt defamiliarization and the consequent transformation of conventional feelings and concepts. In this way, we have been able to articulate a model that can be subjected to empirical study. In general, the literary features we have mentioned are identifiable in relation to the norms of language or narrative that are apparent in ordinary discourse (e.g., the language and narrative forms used in newspaper articles), but they may also occur in relation to local norms created by a prevailing style or narrative strategy within the text itself. Hunt and Vipond's (1986) discourse evaluations, for example, are noticed because they stand out from local text norms.

In the literary context, readers find these variations striking and evocative. Although such features also may occur in ordinary prose, albeit less frequently, in that context they tend to convey meanings that are incongruent with the situation model overtly developed in the text—and readers are likely to ignore them. However, for literary readers, attention is captured and held, and, for a moment, familiar and conventionally understood referents seem less familiar, as though there is something "more" to them than can be immediately grasped (defamiliarization). In response, as readers reflect on the implications of a defamiliarizing expression, their reinterpretive effort modifies or transforms their conventional feelings or concepts. Such reinterpretation usually follows an interval during which readers search (not necessarily consciously) for an appropriate context within which to locate or generate such new understanding. Our empirical studies indicate that feeling is the primary vehicle for this search.

It is, of course, possible to read a text in a literary manner despite the absence of foregrounded stylistic or narrative features; that is, a "found poem" or a newspaper article might be presented to readers as literary. A well-known demonstration of this point is provided by Fish's (1980) anecdote of the "poem" on the blackboard: Actually consisting of the names of five literary critics, his students were ready to interpret this as a poem when instructed to do so. Similarly, Zwaan's (1993) studies have shown that, when readers are led to believe that a text is literary (even though some of his excerpts were from newspaper articles), they read more slowly and recalled more of the surface details of the text than did readers who encountered the same text believing that it was from a newspaper. Although such reader behavior also would be expected in response to a text containing foregrounding, we suggest that these behaviors do not constitute actual literary reading. Without encountering significant foregrounded passages, Zwaan's readers were unlikely to have experienced the defamiliarization and the modification or transformation of conventional feelings or concepts specified by our model. In sum, atypical cases such as Fish's anecdote or Zwaan's newspaper readers are suggestive but marginal, offering an insufficient basis on which to found a theory of literary reading.

Thus, we suggest that literariness conceived as a transforming process is not merely conventional, the result of acculturation; it is not the result of a control process, put in place by previous experience with literary genres, although knowledge of such genres may facilitate reading once a text is recognized as literary. Rather, literariness at its most fundamental level is an outcome of our psychobiological inheritance that involves linguistic capabilities, feeling expression, and self-perception. Drawing on these capacities, literary response plays a critical role in alerting us to alternative perspectives on our selves and on our social and natural environments. Several aspects of this view challenge contemporary conceptions of literary response. In what follows, we look critically at two representative examples of such contemporary frameworks and confront them with some empirical evidence for the distinctiveness of literary reading. Our first example is taken from the arguments of a postmodern critic, Barbara Herrnstein Smith, in *Contingencies of Value* (1988).

## THE STABILITY OF LITERARINESS

Like other contemporary critics, such as Fish (1980, 1989) and Eagleton (1983), Smith (1988) is most concerned about the meaning and value of literary texts. How does literature come to have the value it does, inspiring us to give it the careful interpretive attention that we do? According to Smith, literary value is determined extrinsically, as a product of historical circumstances; what is deemed of value in one epoch may well be valued quite differently or not at all in another (cf. Eagleton, 1983, pp. 10–11). In this view, all aspects of evaluative judgments are dependent on the social position of the evaluator; nothing is dependent on the qualities of the work of art itself: "There are no functions performed by artworks that may be specified as generically unique" (Smith, 1988, p. 35). To the extent that a reader identifies features or properties of a work for attention, these are "the variable products of the subject's engagement with his or her environment under a particular set of conditions" (pp. 31–32). Thus, we are asked to suppose that the reader we cited earlier singles out the metaphor in Coleridge's line because she has been subjected to educational practices that promote such activities and valorize the states of mind that result.

Smith (1988) suggested that those in control of aesthetic judgment (usually in academia) expect texts to perform the functions they find proper or desirable, finding any other functions irrelevant or improper. This controlling group is also said to deem necessary the conditions under which its members engage literary texts, whereas other conditions are considered irregular or substandard (p. 41). However, this imputes much more power to the "controlling" group than it actually possesses; our own empirical studies of student readers, such as the reader we have cited, show far more divergent reading practices and varied understandings of literature than Smith's account would allow. In their interpretations and evaluations, actual readers go their own way, especially when unconstrained by classroom structures of authority.

Nonetheless, these readers' diverse construals of meaning are neither irresponsible nor whimsical, as is sometimes suggested (Fish, 1989, p. 83; Smith, 1988, p. 11). We have been able to demonstrate in several ways that the formal, stylistic features of literary texts persistently influence the reading process—even when readers' interpretations and valuations are highly variable. For example, we have coded the segments of a short story (usually one sentence) for the presence of stylistic features, that is, foregrounding (Mukařovský, 1932/1964). When we ask readers to read the story, we invariably find a substantial correlation between the amount of foregrounding and the reading time for each segment as well as significant correlations between foregrounding and readers' ratings of each segment for strikingness, feeling, and uncertainty. That is, readers spend more time reading segments high in foregrounding, and they find those segments more striking, evocative of more feeling, and productive of greater uncertainty (Miall & Kuiken, 1994b). Because these relations are found whether the readers are students of literature or students with little or no current interest in reading literature, this is evidence that the response to foregrounding is independent of literary training (Steen, 1994; van Peer, 1986).

The role of foregrounded features in transcending the readers' cultural background is also suggested by another study, based on Coleridge's long poem "The Rime of the Ancient Mariner" (Coleridge, 1817/1924). Here, taking the extensive critical literature on the poem from 1900 to 1991, we counted the occurrence of quotations from the poem's 625 lines in 166 articles and book chapters. Then, during the study from which we have already cited one reader's comments (Sikora et al., 1998), 30 readers nominated and commented on five passages that they found striking. The correspondence between the frequency with which lines were selected from the poem by the critics and by the student readers was assessed: This correlation was substantial and highly significant, $r(623) = .44, p < .0001$. Informally, we observed that, for both groups, the most frequently selected lines of the poem either were high in foregrounding or captured moments of considerable narrative importance (with ambivalent or multivalent meanings). Passages from the poem apparently have the power to attract attention in ways that transcend time (1900–1991), literary experience (student or critic), or critical perspective (psychoanalytic, new historicist, etc.).

Smith (1988) argued, in contrast, that it is a mistake to attribute commonalities in response to

> fundamental "traits," recurrent "features," or shared "properties" of valued works. The attempt to locate invariance in the nature (or, latterly, the *structure*) of the works themselves is ... no less misguided than the search for essential or objective value—and is, in fact, only another form of that search. (p. 15)

Thus, Smith (characteristically among postmodern theorists) regards the identification of features in a literary text that directs reader response to be a form of essentialism. In her account, the "properties" or "features" of a text are "at every point the variable products of particular subjects' interactions with it" (p. 48). There can be no fixed, determinate features influencing all readers. These, when they appear, flow from the valuations enforced on readers by what Fish (1980) called the interpretive community; they are a product of educational and cultural norms.

It is quite true, as Smith (1988) said, that "literary value is not the property of an object *or* a subject but, rather, *the product of the dynamics of a system*" (p. 15). However, she went on to claim: "As readers and critics of literature, we are within that system"; thus, because we "have particular interests, we will, at any given moment, be viewing it from *some* perspective" (p. 16). What is missing from this account, we suggest, is that these interests, in part, follow from literary reading rather than shaping it in advance. So, regardless of interpretive community, a reader will regularly notice distinctive stylistic and narrative features in a text and find them strikingly (i.e., evocatively) defamiliarizing. In this respect, the reader's conventional perspective does not direct the reading experience. On the contrary, it is precisely the conventional perspective of the reader that the literariness of the text calls into question. In our first example, for instance, the reader of Coleridge's (1817/1924) "The Nightingale" brought to the reading situation her prior and conventional perspective on time—and found this perspective unsettled by the opening lines of the poem. If our interests were invariably in control, as Smith supposed, these strikingly defamiliarizing passages in literary texts would be inconceivable.

The strikingness of literature occurs against a background of familiarity and habituation. During literary reading, the perspectives that we have, perhaps unthinkingly, acquired from our culture are especially likely to be questioned. If so, this points to the adaptive value of literature in reshaping our perspectives and providing us with greater flexibility, especially by impelling us to reconsider our system of convictions and values. Although the processes embodied by foregrounding and defamiliarization have been central to literary theorists from the time of the Romantic theorists, such as Coleridge and Shelley, Cook (1994, p. 10) is one of the few contemporary theorists of discourse analysis to put forward, as we do (Miall, 1989), schema refreshment as a characteristic component of literary response. Our proposal, as we show later, diverges from Cook's in accommodating the role of feeling, which we see as central to the reinterpretive processes evoked by literary texts.

## BEYOND THE NARRATIVE SITUATION

The difficulty of identifying and understanding what, if anything, is distinctive about the response to literature is also apparent in recent studies of discourse processing. In this section, we refer briefly to two important studies of narrative comprehension (Trabasso & Magliano, 1996; Zwaan, Magliano, & Graesser, 1995) and show their relation to the conception of literariness that we have proposed. Our aim is to suggest that, despite the technical sophistication of discourse processing theory (Graesser, Millis, & Zwaan, 1997), literariness involves processes that appear beyond the power of this approach to explain (cf. Miall & Kuiken, 1994a). These processes may include, but almost certainly go beyond, the particular "control processes" that Zwaan (1993, 1996) proposed to account for the "inconsiderate" nature of literary texts.

Apart from Zwaan's (1993, 1996) proposal, which is situated within Kintsch's (1988) construction–integration model, the goal of discourse processing theory has been to articulate the processes by which readers comprehend all texts, whether expository or narrative. Van Dijk (1979), for example, saw no issues unique to literary comprehension and urged its absorption into a general theory of discourse processing. More recently, in their elaboration of the situation model perspective, authors such as Zwaan and Radvansky (1998) assumed that understanding the situation model in a narrative text is "tantamount to the successful comprehension of a text" (p. 162). This we show, is by no means clear; current studies of how readers form situation models have failed to address the significant contributions of literariness to the reading process.

Zwaan and his colleagues (Zwaan, Langston, & Graesser, 1995; Zwaan, Magliano, et al., 1995) provided persuasive evidence of the reader's construction of a situation model during response to narrative. Construction of a situation model consists of the processing of arguments (or propositions) and their relations (connections between referents) to address different components of situational continuity, such as temporality, spatiality, and causality. When segments of a short story are coded for continuities and discontinuities in these components, the prediction of reading times using multiple regression techniques can be used to indicate the processing requirements for constructing the situation model (Zwaan, Magliano, et al., 1995). A situation model, however, represents the array of cognitive processes necessary for understanding any narrative. It is this perspective that literary narratives, with their defamiliarizing power, seem particularly likely to challenge.

Although certain stylistic variations, such as some forms of temporal deviation, may be captured by the situation model, the broader array of foregrounded features falls outside its scope. To examine this possibility, we reanalyzed responses to one of the stories studied by Zwaan, Magliano, and Graesser (1995), Elizabeth Bowen's (1981) "The Demon Lover." The segments of the story, as determined by Zwaan et al., were coded for foregrounding. For example, in the sentence, "She stopped dead and stared at the hall table," we noted the occurrence of the repeated *st* sound, the pair of adjacent stresses on both *stopped dead* and *hall table* (which slows the rate of reading), and the metaphoric term *dead,* which, although a conventional expression, begins to seem ominous in the context of the story. Our count of such features at the phonetic, grammatical, and semantic levels, converted to standard scores and summed, constituted the code for foregrounding for this sentence. We have previously found that a higher score predicts longer reading times (Miall & Kuiken, 1994b).

The foregrounding code and the codes for the situation model (i.e., temporal, spatial, and causal discontinuities) were then compared as predictors of the reading times obtained by Zwaan, Magliano, and Graesser (1995) in a regression model in which variation among items served as the error term. In the regression model, we also included *perspective* (a code representing degree of proximity to the point of view and feelings of the main character, explained in detail later), new arguments and argument overlap (to control for the number of new propositional text base nodes), the serial position of the sentences (to control for the typical increase in reading speed as readers progress through a story), and the syllable count per segment (to control for segment length). Although the overall model was, as expected, very significant, $F(9, 139) = 183.24$, $p < .0001$, of greater importance is evidence that the independent contribution of foregrounding to the prediction of reading time was comparable to that for new arguments and greater than that for any of the theoretical components of the situation model (see Table 1). We also tested a hierarchical regression model in which serial position of the sentences, syllable count per segment, new arguments, and argument overlap were entered in the first step; the theoretical variables for the situation model and perspective were entered in the second step; and foregrounding was entered in the third step. We found that the theoretical variables for the situation model and perspective contributed 35% and that foregrounding contributed 65% of the increase in explained variance beyond that accounted for by the first block of variables.

TABLE 1
Correlations Between Individual Variables and Mean Reading Times Following Multiple Regression Analysis of Story Factors for "The Demon Lover"

| Variable | Simple | Partial |
| --- | --- | --- |
| Segment | –0.15 | –0.21** |
| Syllables | 0.94**** | 0.84**** |
| New arguments | 0.72**** | 0.30**** |
| Argument overlap | 0.11 | –0.07 |
| Time | 0.14 | 0.16* |
| Space | 0.13 | 0.08 |
| Cause | 0.24*** | 0.06 |
| Perspective | 0.21** | –0.01 |
| Foregrounding | 0.72**** | 0.26**** |

Note. $df = 147$.
*$p < .05$. **$p < .025$. ***$p < .01$. ****$p < .005$ (all $p$ values are one-tailed).

What are the implications of these findings for our conception of how readers understand literary texts? How does the response to foregrounding relate to the pattern of inferences commonly analyzed in discourse studies? These questions can be pursued further by examining think-aloud protocols gathered while people read a literary story. Our approach to this task may be compared to the strategy of Trabasso and Magliano (1996), who outlined a theoretical approach to analyzing readers' verbal comments in response to a simple story (a very short narrative about Ivan the warrior who kills a marauding dragon). They showed that the inferences generated by their readers fell into one of three categories: backward looking (explanation), concurrent (associations), or forward looking (predictions). Explanation is backward oriented because it serves "to unite the focal sentence with either text information or prior knowledge-based inferences" (p. 259). Explanations are concerned with the reasons why something occurs; they refer to "external states, events, goals and other internal states, emotional reactions, actions, and outcomes that signal goal success or failure" (p. 259). In other words, explanations provide the physical, motivational, and psychological causes, or enabling conditions" (p. 259) to understand a given episode. Explanations are the most common type of comment in the protocols analyzed in their study. The frequency of comments was as follows: explanations, 50%; associations, 16%; predictions, 9%; metacomments, 4%; and paraphrases, 21%.

In comparison, in a study of responses to a literary story, the think-aloud protocols that we analyzed (Kuiken & Miall, 1995) contained a somewhat lower proportion of explanations—as well as a variety of other categories not envisaged by Trabasso and Magliano (1996). The story, "The Trout" by Seán O'Faoláin (1980), was divided into 84 segments (usually one sentence), which 30 participants read one at a time on a computer screen. As they read, they commented on their changing understanding of the story. The resulting think-aloud protocols were analyzed into constituents, using methods in which recurrent expressions of similar meanings across protocols, rather than theory, determined the categories that were formed (Kuiken, Schopflocher, & Wild, 1989). For this analysis, the resulting constituents were grouped into 14 types: These are shown with example constituents in Table 2. The frequency of constituents of each type was also compiled for each of the 84 story segments.

As shown in the left-hand section of Table 3, explanations of character actions were the most common type of constituent; if these are added to the more general elaborative explanations made by participants, explanations accounted for approximately 36% of the total comments. Although our principles for coding types of comments differed from those of Trabasso and Magliano (1996), the broad categories are sufficiently similar to compare our proportions with theirs. Besides the relatively few explanations, it should be noted that our story elicited fewer associative and anticipatory comments. Most noteworthy, however, is the large number of comments that are arguably distinctive to the process of literary reading:

TABLE 2
Types of Comment in Analyses of Think-Aloud Protocols
for "The Trout," With Example Comments

| Types of Comments | Examples |
|---|---|
| Character explanation | Julia will do it again for the excitement |
| Elaborative explanation | The problem of the trout is still unresolved |
| Association | The tunnel is dark and cold |
| Anticipation | Julia will throw the trout in the river |
| World knowledge | The Dark Walk could be in Britain or Newfoundland |
| Quotations | "Cool ooze of the river's bank" |
| Style | I notice the use of a simile in describing the fish |
| Imagery | I get an image of the scene of the trout |
| Query | I wonder if Julia is afraid or does not want to get caught |
| Surprise | I am struck that the trout is described as "panting" |
| Reader emotion | I am glad Julia is troubled |
| Thematizing | Again, we have the symbolism of the trout in a prison |
| Literary reference | The character's dialect reminds me of *Wuthering Heights* |
| Reading awareness | It's easy to get involved in the story from the beginning |

1. Readers frequently appear to be struck by the surface code of the story, prompting them to repeat phrases verbatim while reading (21.5% of comments).
2. They are alert to formal features of the text, commenting rather often on stylistic aspects of the story (7.6%).
3. They often find the story puzzling or unclear, leading to a high proportion of queries about meaning (10.1%).
4. They sometimes express surprise in response to story elements (4.1%).
5. They occasionally formulate interpretive ideas while reading, an activity we have termed *thematizing* (3.1%).

Literary readers thus undertake interpretive activities not generally accounted for in the discourse processing tradition, even when a literary narrative is under consideration (as in Zwaan, Magliano, et al., 1995). To determine the origins of such comments, the frequency (per segment) of each type of comment was correlated with other variables, following the "three-pronged" approach advocated by Graesser et al. (1997). First, we created a set of theoretical variables that we expected would predict readers' think-aloud comments. Each segment was coded for the occurrence of foregrounded features, as described earlier (i.e., a count of stylistic features at the phonetic, grammatical, and semantic levels). Next, the story segments were coded for the new arguments and situation model variables, following the method of Zwaan, Magliano, et al. (1995); of these, the new argu-

TABLE 3
Frequency of Types of Commentary in Talk-Aloud Protocols for "The Trout," With Correlations by Segment With Story and Reader Variables

| | | | Partial Correlations (Controlling for Syllables) | | | | | |
| | | | Story Variables | | | Reader Variables | | |
| Protocol Types | Scored[a] | % | Foreground | New Arguments | Perspective | Reading Time | Uncertainty | Importance |
|---|---|---|---|---|---|---|---|---|
| Character explanation | 861 | 33.6 | -.179 | -.171 | .262* | -.069 | -.099 | .154 |
| Elaborative explanation | 53 | 2.1 | .085 | .051 | -.069 | -.141 | -.078 | -.063 |
| Association | 166 | 6.5 | .289** | .159 | -.230* | .402*** | .248** | -.163 |
| Anticipation | 84 | 3.3 | .068 | -.029 | .031 | -.007 | .033 | .145 |
| World knowledge | 95 | 3.7 | .045 | .171 | -.170 | .083 | -.080 | -.393*** |
| Quotations | 551 | 21.5 | .463*** | .173 | .186 | .205* | .304** | -.092 |
| Style | 194 | 7.6 | .301** | .284** | .039 | .387*** | .400*** | -.062 |
| Imagery | 39 | 1.5 | .228* | .204* | -.079 | .061 | .106 | -.155 |
| Query | 258 | 10.1 | .167 | .198 | .042 | .438*** | .596*** | .230* |
| Surprise | 106 | 4.1 | .339** | .106 | .220* | .193 | .334** | .109 |
| Reader emotion | 80 | 3.1 | -.150 | -.069 | -.064 | -.071 | -.097 | .049 |
| Thematizing | 55 | 2.1 | -.112 | .110 | .228* | -.045 | .042 | .240* |
| Literary reference | 15 | 0.6 | | | | | | |
| Reading awareness | 4 | 0.2 | | | | | | |
| | | | Intercorrelation of Story and Reader Variables | | | | | |
| New arguments | | | .013 | — | | | | |
| Perspective | | | .259* | -.122 | — | | | |
| Reading time | | | .414*** | .322** | .151 | — | | |
| Uncertainty | | | .355*** | .195 | .263** | .463*** | — | |
| Importance | | | .047 | -.150 | .368*** | -.035 | .141 | — |

[a]2,561 segment constituents out of 3,183 were scored (80.5%); the remaining constituents were based on sections of the story larger than the segment.
*$p < .05$. **$p < .01$. ***$p < .001$ (all $p$ values are one-tailed).

ments' variable proved the most robust predictor and is the only variable reported here. In addition, because the literary story we used centers primarily on a single character (a young girl called Julia), we created a 4-point scale for perspective, assessing the reader's degree of intimacy with this character. This scale ranged from 1 (*no reference to character*), through 2 (*external views of her behavior*), through 3 (*descriptions of the character's cognitions*), to 4 (*the invitation to share her perspective or feelings through free indirect discourse*; Miall & Kuiken, in press).

In the upper portion of Table 3, we present partial correlations (controlling for segment length) between the frequency of each type of comment and the scores for each of these three story variables. It is noteworthy that foregrounding most powerfully predicts the frequency of associative comments, quotations, comments on style, and expressions of surprise. New arguments most powerfully predict comments on style and imagery, suggesting the contribution of novel propositions to the vividness with which narrative events can be imagined. Perspective, on the other hand, is systematically related to explanations of character: The closer readers feel to Julia the more they seem impelled to formulate explanations for her behavior.

In a parallel study (Miall & Kuiken, 1994b), we collected reading times per segment from 60 readers who read "The Trout" at their normal pace. Readers then reread the story, and different groups provided one type of rating (e.g., strikingness, uncertainty, or importance) for each story segment. In Table 3, we show correlations with reading times and two of the ratings, those for uncertainty (how uncertain readers were about the meaning of a given segment) and those for importance (how important to the meaning of the story the reader considered a given segment). Here, in contrast with the report by Trabasso and Magliano (1996, p. 263) that the number of explanations predicts reading times, it is the production of associations, comments on style, and queries that predict longer reading times. The ratings for uncertainty suggest why this is so; the production of associations, comments on style, and queries also predict uncertainty (as do the number of quotations and expressions of surprise). Uncertainty, in other words, appears to signal an increased demand on processing resources that is characteristic of literary response. In this regard, it is important to note that uncertainty also correlates with the occurrence of foregrounding, as the intercorrelations in the lower half of Table 3 indicate.

The pattern of findings shown in this study and the previous study, in which we reanalyzed responses to "The Demon Lover," point to the power of foregrounding as a major influence on literary readers. In addition, the second study suggests that, if the result of the encounter with foregrounding is defamiliarization, that is, putting in question prior concepts or feelings, the resulting uncertainty creates a distinctive "control condition" for literary understanding. This is a rather different conception, however, than the control system envisaged by Zwaan (1993, 1996). Although uncertainty may contribute to delaying formation of a situation model, as Zwaan proposed, our perspective suggests that uncertainty, more significantly, heralds the transformations in understanding that occur during the reader's thematization of the literary text. As we have argued elsewhere (Miall, 1995; Miall & Kuiken, 1994a, 1994b), it is during this process that feeling seems likely to play a critical role. As the vehicle of interpretation, guiding the "effort after meaning" (Bartlett, 1932, p. 44), feeling initiates a process in which existing schemata become recontextualized, leading to new insights for the reader. It is this process that we examine in the last section of this article.

## TRANSFORMATIONS OF PERSONAL MEANINGS

The components of the situation model, and the inferential processes that support it, represent aspects of comprehension that are probably obligatory for all readers. Similarly, the relation between foregrounding and defamiliarization is evident regardless of literary training (Miall & Kuiken, 1994b), orientation toward reading, or personality characteristics (Miall & Kuiken, 1995). In contrast, the reinterpretive effort that follows defamiliarization seems to be the source of individual differences in response to literary texts. We have consistently found that foregrounding evokes feeling (Miall & Kuiken, 1994b), and evidence emerging from our studies indicates that feeling provides a route to the self, especially to personal experiences that offer a new interpretive context following the moment of defamiliarization. The modification or transformation of readers' concepts or feelings, the third component of literariness that we introduced earlier, is thus specific to the individual reader: It is in this respect, indeed, that literature seems to invoke what is individual in the individual.

A second example from the same participant in the "Mariner" study shows how this process unfolds in a mode of response (shown in only one group of protocols from this study) that we call *enactment* because it seems to involve actively living through a particular experience consequent on reading (for a more complete account, see Sikora et al., 1998). The verse selected by the reader comes late in the poem:

> Like one, that on a lonesome road
> Doth walk in fear and dread,
> And having once turned round walks on,
> And turns no more his head;
> Because he knows, a frightful fiend
> Doth close behind him tread.
>
> (Coleridge, 1817/1924, p. 203)

I'm just going to share the emotion of being alone, in the dark, with this threat. Knowing that there's nothing you can do about it, keeping on walking and pretending it's not happening, just because there's no other way to cope with it, you can't run from it. . . . I also sense there's no point in fighting this because, like it's a guilt thing, he's the one that's responsible for what's happened, he's the reason that this thing is following him, so there is no point in trying to get away from it because, it's your fate. It's just a bit of a reminder that everybody dies. Whatever's following him is going to get him. You don't know how long it's going to go and you don't know when it's going to get him, but you know that eventually it will.

After exploring the feeling of being alone, the reader turns to the situation of the protagonist ("it's a guilt thing, he's the one that's responsible") and then makes an important generalization that seems to include herself. In this way, the response unfolds in successive phases: Initial awareness of a feeling with some personal relevance, the use of this feeling to locate a meaning for the poem, and the application of this notion to the position of the protagonist. Finally, in what is perhaps the most interesting part of the commentary, we see a convergence of the protagonist's situation with that of the reader: The "he" and "you" appear to become interchangeable. Although "this thing is following *him*," "it's *your* fate." The story understanding that emerges at this point appears to be "everybody dies." Although this is certainly not a profound insight in itself, the way in which it is reached has made it personal to the reader and enabled her to pursue a particular theme that seems to have concerned her throughout her reading of the poem (her first comment was, "I seem to be picking on a bit of a theme of threatening").

We also found traces of enactive reading among some readers in the think-aloud study of the Seán O'Faoláin story (Kuiken & Miall, 1995). One group of readers, who frequently commented on stylistic and narrative features of the story, also consistently identified characters' thoughts (e.g., their doubts and preoccupations), anthropomorphized nonhuman "characters" in the story (referring to their loneliness and fear), and repeatedly attributed a mood to story settings. These same readers revisited the connotations of story elements, frequently bestowing story events with universal significance in relation to the "general pattern of life," the "tensions between life and death," and so on. These observations are consistent with the notion that feelings evoked by defamiliarizing story features permeated these readers' interpretive—and enactive—engagement with the story. Although space does not permit their review here, other studies undertaken in our laboratory indicate that this aspect of literariness emerges especially among depressed persons who have recently experienced loss (Kuiken, Miall, & Meunier, 1996) and among readers who are predisposed to read literary texts for insight (Kuiken, Miall, Busink, & Cey, 1996).

In conclusion, the first two components of literariness, which include stylistic features or striking features due to narrative, and the reader's defamiliarizing response to them, are necessary but insufficient to identify literariness. The third component is constituted by the reader's attempts to articulate the phenomena within the text that are found striking and evocative of feeling. These attempts may be expressed in the type of comment that we earlier called thematizing. Enactive readers progressively transform an affective theme across striking or evocative passages, becoming implicated in the existential concerns embodied in those passages.

We suggest that the conception of literariness can appropriately be grounded in this three-level analysis. The third level is the least well understood and will require further carefully designed research studies (cf. Miall & Kuiken, in press). However, we believe that future empirical study is likely to show that these interacting components of literary response are not only distinctive but also rest on a unique configuration of psychological and somatic responses. This, in the last analysis, is what gives literary response its enduring power in human cultural evolution.

## ACKNOWLEDGMENTS

The research reported here was supported in part by Program Grant 53–10128 from the Social Sciences and Humanities Research Council of Canada. The first version of this article was presented at the Sixth Biannual IGEL Conference, Utrecht, The Netherlands, August 1998. We thank Rolf Zwaan for supplying the data from Zwaan, Magliano, and Graesser (1995) that forms part of the analysis reported here. Our particular thanks go to Kees van Rees, whose persistent questions led us to formulate this response to the problem of what constitutes literariness, and to the three reviewers of this article whose trenchant comments on an earlier draft helped us to clarify our arguments.

## REFERENCES

Bartlett, F. C. (1932). *Remembering: A study in experimental and social psychology.* Cambridge, England: Cambridge University Press.

Bowen, E. (1981). The demon lover. In C Brown (Ed.), *The collected stories of Elizabeth Bowen* (pp. 661–666). New York: Knopf.

Coleridge, S. T. (1924). *The poems of Samuel Taylor Coleridge* (E. H. Coleridge, Ed.). Oxford, England: Oxford University Press. (Original work published 1817)

Cook, G. (1994). *Discourse and literature: The interplay of form and mind.* Oxford, England: Oxford University Press.

Eagleton, T. (1983). *Literary theory: An introduction.* Oxford, England: Basil Blackwell.

Erlich, V. (1981). *Russian formalism: History—Doctrine* (3rd ed.). New Haven, CT: Yale University Press.

Fish, S. (1980). *Is there a text in this class? The authority of interpretive communities.* Cambridge, MA: Harvard University Press.

Fish, S. (1989). *Doing what comes naturally: Change, rhetoric, and the practice of theory in literary and legal studies.* Durham, NC: Duke University Press.

Graesser, A. C., Millis, K. K., & Zwaan, R. A. (1997). Discourse comprehension. *Annual Review of Psychology, 48,* 163–189.
Hobbs, J. R. (1990). *Literature and cognition.* Stanford, CA: Center for the Study of Language and Information.
Hunt, R. A., & Vipond, D. (1986). Evaluations in literary reading. *Text, 6,* 53–71.
Kintsch, W. (1988). The role of knowledge in discourse comprehension: A construction–integration model. *Psychological Review, 95,* 163–182.
Kuiken, D., & Miall, D. S. (1995). Procedures in think aloud studies: Contributions to the phenomenology of literary response. In G. Rusch (Ed.), *Empirical approaches to literature: Proceedings of the Fourth Biannual Conference of the International Society for the Empirical Study of Literature, IGEL* (pp. 50–60). Siegen, Germany: LUMIS-Publications.
Kuiken, D., Miall, D. S., Busink, R., & Cey, R. (1996, August). *Aesthetic attitude and insight-oriented reading: The realization of personal meanings in literary texts.* Paper presented at the conference of the International Association for Empirical Aesthetics, Prague, The Czech Republic.
Kuiken, D., Miall, D. S., & Meunier, R. (1996, August). *Loss, depression, and feeling realization during reading.* Paper presented at the conference of the International Society for the Empirical Study of Literature, IGEL, Banff, Canada.
Kuiken, D., Schopflocher, D., & Wild, T. C. (1989). Numerically aided phenomenology: A demonstration. *Journal of Mind and Behavior, 10,* 373–392.
Miall, D. S. (1989). Beyond the schema given: Affective comprehension of literary narratives. *Cognition and Emotion, 3,* 55–78.
Miall, D. S. (1995). Anticipation and feeling in literary response: A neuropsychological perspective. *Poetics, 23,* 275–298.
Miall, D. S., & Kuiken, D. (1994a). Beyond text theory: Understanding literary response. *Discourse Processes, 17,* 337–352.
Miall, D. S., & Kuiken, D. (1994b). Foregrounding, defamiliarization, and affect: Response to literary stories. *Poetics, 22,* 389–407.
Miall, D. S., & Kuiken, D. (1995). Aspects of literary response: A new questionnaire. *Research in the Teaching of English, 29,* 37–58.
Miall, D. S., & Kuiken, D. (1998). The form of reading: Empirical studies of literariness. *Poetics, 25,* 327–341.
Miall, D. S., & Kuiken, D. (in press). Shifting perspectives: Readers' feelings and literary response. In W. van Peer & S. Chatman (Eds.), *New perspectives on narrative perspective.* Albany: State University of New York Press.
Mukařovský, J. (1964). Standard language and poetic language. In P. L. Garvin (Ed.), *A Prague School reader on esthetics, literary structure, and style* (pp. 17–30). Washington, DC: Georgetown University Press. (Original work published 1932)
O'Faoláin, S. (1980). The trout. In *The collected stories of Seán O'Faoláin* (pp. 383–386). London: Constable.
Sikora, S., Kuiken, D., & Miall, D. S. (1998, August). *Enactment versus interpretation: A phenomenological study of readers' responses to Coleridge's "The Rime of the Ancient Mariner."* Paper presented at the sixth biannual conference of the International Society for the Empirical Study of Literature, IGEL, Utrecht, The Netherlands. (Available online at: http://www.lumis.uni-siegen.de/igel/en/igelconf/c1998/sikora.pdf)
Smith, B. H. (1988). *Contingencies of value: Alternative perspectives for critical theory.* Cambridge, MA: Harvard University Press.
Steen, G. (1994). *Understanding metaphor in literature.* London: Longman.
Trabasso, T., & Magliano, J. P. (1996). Conscious understanding during comprehension. *Discourse Processes, 21,* 255–287.
van Dijk, T. (1979). Advice on theoretical poetics. *Poetics, 8,* 569–608.
van Peer, W. (1986). *Stylistics and psychology: Investigations of foregrounding.* London: Croom Helm.

Zholkovsky, A. (1984). *Themes and texts: Toward a poetics of expressiveness.* Ithaca, NY: Cornell University Press.

Zwaan, R. A. (1993). *Aspects of literary comprehension.* Amsterdam: Benjamins.

Zwaan, R. A. (1996). Toward a model of literary comprehension. In B. K. Britton & A. C. Graesser (Eds.), *Models of understanding text* (pp. 241–255). Mahwah, NJ: Lawrence Erlbaum Associates, Inc.

Zwaan, R. A., Langston, M. C., & Graesser, A. C. (1995). The construction of situation models in narrative comprehension: An event-indexing model. *Psychological Science, 6,* 292–297.

Zwaan, R. A., Magliano, J. P., & Graesser, A. C. (1995). Dimensions of situation model construction in narrative comprehension. *Journal of Experimental Psychology: Learning, Memory, and Cognition, 21,* 386–397.

Zwaan, R. A., & Radvansky, G. A. (1998). Situation models in language comprehension and memory. *Psychological Bulletin, 123,* 162–185.

# Metaphorical (In)Coherence in Discourse

## Yeshayahu Shen and Noga Balaban
*The Program of Cognitive Studies of Language and Its Uses*
*Tel Aviv University*
*Tel Aviv, Israel*

This article introduces a critique of a version of the conceptual metaphor (CM) view (e.g., Lakoff & Johnson, 1980), regarding the issue of metaphorical coherence in natural discourse. The issue at stake is: Are metaphorical expressions in natural discourse coherently or incoherently distributed in discourse? The hypothesis derived from the theories developed by certain proponents of the CM view is that the occurrence of a conventional metaphorical expression (e.g., "We have reached a crossroads in our relationship") that instantiates a certain root or conceptual conventional metaphor (e.g., *LOVE IS A JOURNEY*) will support the use of consistent metaphorical expressions, that is, expressions belonging with the same root metaphors (e.g., "Let's change direction"). In this study, we compared 15 randomly selected passages taken from daily newspapers to a baseline of 15 newspaper passages that marked their deliberate, explicit use of an underlying root metaphor. Contrary to the prediction derived from (a certain version of) the CM view, we found significant differences between the 2 samples. These findings are discussed in light of a recent debate over the role played by conceptual metaphors in language use.

Traditionally, the study of metaphor, especially in the cognitive sciences, has focused on the analysis of individual examples, asking questions such as, How do we identify an expression as a metaphor? How do we interpret it? And so forth. The issue of the relation between metaphorical expressions and their distribution in authentic natural discourse, and what this may tell us about metaphorical thought, has been virtually ignored. Hardly any attention has been paid to the question of whether the extensive set of metaphorical expressions that occur in any discourse cohere in any systematic or structured manner. Recently, however, the issue has become a central concern within the framework of arguably one of the most influential theories of metaphor to have been proposed during the last 20

---

Correspondence and requests for reprints should be sent to Yeshayahu Shen, Department of Poetics and Comparative Literature, Tel Aviv University, 69978 Tel Aviv, Israel. E-mail: yshen@taunivm.bitnet

years or so, namely, the conceptual metaphor (CM) view as developed by Lakoff and his colleagues (Allbritton, McKoon, & Gerrig, 1995; Lakoff & Gibbs, 1990; Nayak & Gibbs, 1990). This article considers the distribution of metaphors in natural discourse in light of certain implications of this theory to achieve two complementary objectives: to provide an initial study of the relations between metaphors in discourse, and to examine assumptions that are compatible with the CM view of metaphor.

## THE CONCEPTUAL METAPHOR THEORY

A basic tenet of the CM theory is that metaphorical expressions cluster together under conceptual root metaphors. Perhaps the most important insight of Lakoff and Johnson's (1980) highly influential theory of metaphor has been that the metaphorical expressions in ordinary language are systematic and not just one-shot expressions. This systematic nature is related to the idea that various conventional metaphorical expressions (that prevail in ordinary language) are strongly associated with underlying conceptual structures; that is to say, conventional metaphorical expressions cluster together because they share an underlying root metaphor. For example, according to Lakoff and Turner (1989):

> Without such a conceptual metaphor as LIFE IS A JOURNEY, there would be *no conceptual unity* [italics added] to such ordinary conventional expressions as "making one's way in life," "giving one's life some direction," "getting somewhere with one's life," and so on. And there would be no explanation for the use of the same expressions, like "making one's way," "direction," and "getting somewhere," in the domains of both traveling and living. (pp. 116–117; see also Gibbs, 1994)

Other root metaphors registered in Lakoff and Johnson (1980) are *ARGUMENT IS WAR* (as in "Your claims are indefensible" and "His criticisms were right on target") and *IDEAS ARE FOOD* (as in "What he said left a bad taste in my mouth" and "This lecture recycles half-baked ideas").

### The Linguistic Hypothesis: The Use of Conventional Metaphorical Expressions Relies on the Use of Their Underlying Root Metaphor

What role do these root metaphors play in language use and understanding? Ray Gibbs, a major proponent of the CM view, proposed several hypotheses regarding this question (Gibbs, 1994). One of the hypotheses assumes the following role for root metaphors: "Figurative thought functions automatically in people's on-line use and understanding of linguistic meaning" (Gibbs, 1994, p. 18). Let us call this hypothesis *the linguistic hypothesis*. Under this hypothesis, if in a real discourse the conventional expression, "We have reached a crossroads in our relationship," is used, either the production or comprehension of that expression, or both, requires the functional activation and use of the entire root metaphor, *LIFE IS A JOURNEY*. The reason is that such conventional expressions acquire their meanings via their related preexisting metaphor, rather than being directly retrieved from our mental lexicon.

According to Lakoff and Turner (1989): "Without the LIFE IS A JOURNEY metaphor there would be no explanation for how we can understand such poetic expressions as Robert Frost's 'Two roads diverged in a yellow wood'" (pp. 116–117). Gibbs (1994) made a similar point, suggesting that:

> Unlike many theories of metaphor ... the conceptual structure view of metaphor provides an explanation for why so many metaphors are understood effortlessly, without conscious reflection.... Most metaphorical expressions are direct linguistic instantiations of preexisting conceptual mappings between conceptual domains and may thus be understood quite easily during the earliest moments of processing. (p. 251)

Clearly, if many metaphors are understood effortlessly because they rely on preexisting conceptual mappings, this would mean that the very occurrence of a given metaphorical expression reflects the use of that mapping during production and comprehension. This hypothesis is compatible with the CM view but is not necessarily derived from it. As Gibbs (1994) explained, there are other, less radical hypotheses regarding the role that conceptual metaphors can play in language use (e.g., that these metaphors motivate the linguistic meanings that have currency within linguistic communities or that they motivate an individual speaker's use and understanding of why various words and expressions mean what they do). A proponent of the CM view does not have to commit himself or herself to the strongest hypothesis possible. Recently, however, various studies have been conducted (e.g., Allbritton et al., 1995; Gibbs, 1994; Kemper, 1989) in which findings have been interpreted as supporting this hypothesis.

This linguistic hypothesis stands in direct contradiction to the way other theories in psycholinguistics (e.g., Glucksberg & Keysar, 1990; Glucksberg & McGlone, in press) would describe the process of meaning assignment to metaphorical expressions. Consider the expression, "We have reached a crossroads in our relationship." For these theories, the word *crossroad* is a polysemic word in which understanding would require no more than directly accessing the lexical entry for *crossroad* along with ordinary syntactic and pragmatic operations. In contrast, proponents of the linguistic hypothesis would claim that the term *crossroad* is not only a reflection of the metaphorical mapping *LOVE IS A JOURNEY* but also that this root metaphor is functionally activated and used to understand expressions containing this term.

The main difference between the two alternatives, then, pivots on whether the use of conventional expressions requires the functional activation of the underlying root metaphor (as some CM theories would argue) or whether conventional expressions are directly accessed from the mental lexicon without making any recourse to the root metaphor in question, as the "direct access" view would maintain (see Keysar, Shen, & Glucksberg, 1998).

## THE EVIDENCE FOR AND AGAINST THE LINGUISTIC HYPOTHESIS

What evidence can be adduced in support of the linguistic hypothesis? Gibbs (1994, p. 255) presented some of the relevant findings. In general, the evidence that is assumed to support the CM theory rests on the following critical assumption: If people access the relevant root metaphor when they comprehend a certain instantiation of that root metaphor, then it will have a higher facilitation effect for the comprehension of (immediate) subsequent consistent expressions (namely, other instantiations of the same root metaphor) than for inconsistent expressions (i.e., expressions belonging with different root metaphors).

In one study (Allbritton et al., 1995), the reader was provided with texts that contained potential instantiations of a particular mapping. For example, one text stated that "The city's crime epidemic was raging out of control," and it later stated that "Public officials desperately looked for a cure." Both sentences presumably reflect the mapping *CRIME IS A DISEASE*. Using a postcomprehension cued-recognition measure, Allbritton et al. found that recognition of the first sentence was facilitated when cued with the second, suggesting that a link in memory had been established between these two sentences.

Another study (Nayak & Gibbs, 1990, Experiment 6) examined a similar hypothesis regarding the root metaphors underlying idioms. Note that idioms such as "He blew his stack" are said to be motivated by mappings such as *ANGER IS HEATED FLUID IN A CONTAINER*. The researchers presented people with stories that were motivated by this root metaphor, using expressions such as "She was getting hotter with every passing minute" and "As it got closer to five o'clock the pressure was really building up." The participants' task was to judge which of two target idioms represented a more appropriate ending for the preceding scenario. They assumed that:

> If subjects accessed the metaphoric mapping reflected in an idiom's lexical structure, they would interpret *blew her top* as being more appropriate than *bit his head off* even though both phrases are grammatically and conceptually appropriate for the given scenario. (Nayak & Gibbs, 1990, p. 326)

The findings showed that people preferred to complete such texts with idioms that were metaphorically consistent with the earlier ones (e.g., "blew her top") rather than with idioms that were not (e.g., "bit his head off"). These findings and others (e.g., Kemper, 1989) have been taken to support the linguistic hypothesis.

Such studies, however, have been criticized (e.g., Glucksberg & McGlone, in press; Keysar et al., 1998; Kreuz & Graesser, 1991; McGlone, 1996) on the grounds that both the facilitation and inhibition effects reported could be explained by a lexical priming effect rather than by the use of conceptual metaphors. In other words, conventional expressions such as "laid siege" can be said to prime related expressions such as "assault" and "defenses."

Under the "direct access" view, Keysar et al. (1998) suggested that the crucial test for the CM hypothesis cannot depend on whether another conventionalized expression is supported by the preceding conventionalized expressions. Rather, if a conceptual mapping is really being used, then it should be able to support the use of a subsequent novel consistent instantiation as much as it supports the use of consistent conventional instantiations. Participants' reading times were measured for a target sentence that was preceded by one of several scenarios: an implicit mapping scenario (a scenario that made use of several conventional instantiations of the root metaphor), an explicit mapping scenario (a scenario containing an explicit mention of the root metaphor and several novel instantiations of that metaphor), and a literal meaning scenario (for which the target sentence was assigned a literal meaning). It was assumed that the explicit scenario was one in which the root metaphor should be functionally active due to the explicit mention of the root metaphor and the use of novel instantiations. Under the CM view, there should be no facilitation differences between the target sentence in the implicit and explicit conditions because this view assumes that, in both cases, the root metaphor is activated. However, the results showed that target sentences were read faster in literal and novel scenarios than in the implicit scenario. This finding may suggest that no use was made of the root metaphor in the implicit condition and that some additional means (such as the use of novel instantiations) are required for readers to access the root metaphors. Similar findings were obtained by Gentner and Boronat (1992), and Boronat and Gentner (1999). Thus, the empirical evidence at hand does not provide unequivocal support for the linguistic hypothesis made by (some of) the proponents of the CM theory. Note, however, that the rationale underlying all of the aforementioned studies (both those in favor and those against the linguistic hypothesis) was the same. That is, the assumption that, if a certain metaphorical expression in the context supports the comprehension (or enhances the appropriateness) of subsequent consistent expressions (more than it did for nonconsistent expressions), then this may be taken as evidence supporting the hypothesis that the online use of the former relied on the relevant root metaphor.

These studies have focused on the role played by root metaphors in discourse comprehension. However, the CM theory also generates predictions regarding the distribution of metaphorical expressions in natural discourse, as a reflection of the use of root metaphor in the production of discourse (Freeman, 1995; Lakoff & Turner, 1989). In this article, our main goal is to examine the CM view with regard to this aspect of language use, namely, the distribution of metaphorical expressions in natural discourse. We examine this aspect by using a similar rationale to the one that has been applied in the comprehension studies. Under this rationale, the use of a certain root metaphor in comprehending one of its instantiations should facilitate the use of subsequent consistent instantiations. Applying the same logic to the issue of the distribution of metaphorical expressions in discourse, we assume that the use of a given root metaphor in the production of one of its instantiations should support the subsequent use of consistent instantiations. In other words, we assume that the use of a given root metaphor should give rise to subsequent uses of consistent rather than inconsistent instantiations, at least within the boundaries of the same discourse unit (all other things being equal). This prediction can be summarized under the *metaphorical coherence principle,* which can plausibly be derived from the linguistic hypothesis:

> The occurrence of a conventional expression that is linguistically related to a certain conventional root metaphor will support the use of consistent (i.e., compatible) metaphorical expressions (i.e., expressions belonging to the same root metaphor) at least for the immediate discourse unit of discourse.

The major goal of this article is to test this principle with respect to natural discourse.

Clearly, the analysis we are reporting is not an online production analysis. Rather, it constitutes an analysis of the textual products of the (online) production process, that is, the metaphorical expressions that appear in the text. Our assumption is that, if a root metaphor has been used in the production process, it will leave some traces in the pattern of use of these metaphorical expressions. Our goal is to infer from the coherence or incoherence of the relation between these metaphorical expressions whether such activation of the root metaphor has indeed occurred, at a certain point in the production of that discourse. Needless to say, the online production of discourse is a complex process in terms of the various factors that must be involved in it, such that online processing is a separate issue that we will not try to address here. However, we do share with major proponents of the CM view (e.g., Freeman, 1995; Gibbs, 1994; Lakoff & Turner, 1989) the assumption that the metaphorical expressions that appear in natural discourse reflect the use, or lack of use, of the root metaphor(s) that might have motivated such expressions in the first place.

## THE DISTRIBUTION OF METAPHORICAL EXPRESSIONS IN DISCOURSE

The analysis of the distribution of metaphorical expressions in natural discourse as a reflection of the use of root metaphors in the production of discourse has been addressed by proponents of the CM theory (e.g., Freeman, 1995; Lakoff & Turner, 1989). Such studies have, no doubt, made an important contribution to the study of poetic discourse. It is proposed that the metaphorical structure of a given discourse (poetic or nonpoetic) is not only reflected at the linguistic level but at other levels as well. Typically, these studies (e.g., Freeman, 1995) have analyzed either global aspects such as plot units, characters, and themes, or local linguistic units, that is, the selection of metaphorical expressions.

However, none of these studies has provided a systematic examination of the distribution of metaphorical expressions in discourse. The unit of analysis employed in these studies is never defined in theory, and in practice, it varies from linguistic to nonlinguistic units. By contrast, this study seeks systematically to test the metaphorical coherence hypothesis by addressing the question of whether metaphorical expressions are coherently distributed in authentic discourse, as the CM theory of metaphor would predict.

## THE TEXTUAL ANALYSES

### The Research Goals

We intend to examine whether conventional metaphorical expressions are coherently distributed in local units of discourse (e.g., paragraphs), as the metaphorical coherence principle predicts. We will argue that, as far as the distribution of conventional metaphorical expressions in discourse reflects the use of a root metaphor at a certain point in the production of that discourse, these root metaphors are not normally used, in regular or unplanned discourse. To evaluate the level of metaphorical coherence of normal, unplanned pieces of discourse, we need to compare such examples of discourse to some baseline. We have taken pieces of metaphorically planned discourse; that is, discourse that makes deliberate, intended use of a certain root metaphor can be taken as our baseline. Such deliberate use can be marked by various linguistic means indicating the producer's awareness of, and intention to use, a particular root metaphor (e.g., an explicit introduction of the root metaphor in question, such as in the prefatory statement, "Often an argument is like war"). These pieces of planned discourse, then, can provide us with the baseline level of metaphorical coherence that a discourse can achieve when a root metaphor is being used, to which we can compare the level of metaphorical coherence of normal or unplanned pieces of discourse. If the linguistic hypothesis is right, then there should be no difference in the level of metaphorical coherence between the two types because the root metaphor is supposed to be functionally active in both and should therefore generate the same amount of metaphorical coherence. If, however, the alternative view (e.g., the direct access view previously mentioned) is correct, then planned discourse should display a significantly higher level of metaphorical coherence than normal discourse.

Note that the methodology we will be using and, in particular, the use of planned passages as our baseline, to which we compare the unplanned regular discourse, make the inference from the textual products to the use (or lack of use) of root metaphors during the text production a plausible inference. Although there are many factors involved in the production process, these may apply equally to both text types. Therefore, if we can find significant and reliable differences between the level of metaphorical coherence in these two text types, beyond a specific writer or a specific topic, we can ascribe such differences to the activation or nonactivation of the relevant root metaphors rather than to other factors affecting the production process.

## METHOD

### Materials

Fifteen passages, each one paragraph in length (between 100 and 187 words), were randomly selected from 15 different opinion articles dealing with current political issues and events. Each article was written by different authors in the daily newspaper *Ha'aretz*. All passages that contained less than six metaphorical expressions were discarded and replaced by other passages to ensure a minimal number of expressions for the analysis of the degree of metaphorical coherence in each discourse. Fifteen additional passages, which we called *planned paragraphs,* were chosen as the baseline. These passages varied in length from 60 to 461 words and were characterized by various means explicitly marking the producer's deliberate use of some root metaphor throughout the entire passage. Two criteria defined a passage as planned: the inclusion of an explicit statement of the root metaphor in question, and the use of a set (at least three) of novel instantiations belonging with this root metaphor. Explicit mention of the root metaphor was taken to indicate planning because passages do not normally tend to include such a statement of intent. The use of novel instantiations also indicates deliberate use of a root metaphor because their meaning is not conventionally stored in our mental lexicon and can be acquired only on the basis of construction "on the fly" of the root metaphor in question (for an elaboration of this point, see Keysar et al., 1998).

Here is a translation of one of the planned passages used as a baseline in our study (the metaphorical expressions are italicized).

> The Israeli government is a *long dog* with its *tail* in Washington and its head in Jerusalem. Usually the policy of the *long dog* flows from *tail* to *head*. So, usually Rubinstein [head of the Israeli delegation] *wags* Rabin who *shakes* his *head* in Jerusalem from *side to side* to mean that the negotiations are progressing from side to side. When do we know that something has gone wrong? When El-Shafi [head of the Palestinian delegation] *steps* on Rubinstein's *tail* in Washington and we hear an *angry bark* from Jerusalem.

Planned passages such as this were used to determine the level of metaphorical coherence that characterizes discourse that makes deliberate use of a root metaphor. This level of metaphorical coherence then served as a baseline to which we could compare the metaphorical coherence of normal, or unplanned, discourse. If the CM theory is correct, there should be no difference in the degree of metaphorical coherence between the two discourse types because the root metaphor was functionally active in both. If, however, only the planned discourse reflects the true use of a root metaphor, then it should outrank normal discourse with respect to coherence.

## Procedure

To conduct the analysis, we first had to select the metaphorical expressions we were to analyze. This was done as follows: All the metaphorical expressions in each passage were extracted and underwent a twofold classification by two judges. For each expression, the judges explicitly stated the relevant target and source domains, and accordingly, the relevant root metaphor. (Any disagreement between the two judges was resolved by a third judge.) This process resulted in the following:

1. The exclusion of isolated metaphorical expressions for which no conventional root metaphor was identified. Here the judges sought other conventional expressions in Hebrew instantiating the same root metaphor. If no such expressions were found, the expression in question was discarded as being an isolated metaphor.
2. The exclusion of all expressions belonging to ontological or orientational metaphors, following Lakoff and Johnson's (1980) distinction between these and structural metaphors. Ontological and orientational metaphors (e.g., *MORE IS UP, AN IDEA IS AN OBJECT, THE MIND IS A CONTAINER,* etc.) are highly abstract and, therefore, only loosely associated with their instantiations. In contrast, structural metaphors, such as *ARGUMENT IS WAR, LOVE IS A JOURNEY,* and *IDEAS ARE FOOD,* contain far richer conceptual mappings (because they are far more specific) as well as a correspondingly rich repertory of conventional instantiations linked to their root metaphors by strong semantic relations. Structural metaphors, then, represent an appropriate level at which significant and nontrivial relations can be perceived. (Indeed, proponents of the CM theory have typically employed structural metaphors as their experimental materials.)

This procedure yielded the set of all metaphorical expressions to be analyzed in each passage. The average number of metaphorical expressions for the unplanned passages was 10.4, and for the planned ones, 13.5.

## RESULTS AND DISCUSSION

Four analyses were performed: (a) linear coherence, (b) global coherence, (c) global coherence and conventional expressions, and (d) the analysis of alternative expressions to the metaphorical shifts. We discuss each of these in turn.

### Analysis 1: Linear Coherence

The linear coherence of a discourse represents the extent to which successive metaphorical expressions are consistent. It was measured by calculating percentage of shifts versus coherent continuations, out of the total number of transitions from one metaphorical expression to the next, for the same target. For example, if *politics* was metaphorically treated as a building and was followed by another instantiation of the same root metaphor, this was counted as a coherent continuation. If it was followed by an instantiation of a different root metaphor—for example, *POLITICS IS WAR*—this was counted as a shift.

The results were unequivocal. Using a $t$ test for unpaired variables, we found a significant difference between the unplanned and planned discourse types, $p <$ .001. The randomly selected passages yielded an average of 68% shifts ($SD$ = 0.32) and 6% shifts ($SD$ = 0.1), respectively, for the unplanned and planned discourse types. Not only did the planned passages exhibit a much higher degree of linear coherence than the unplanned ones but the former reached (on average) an extremely high degree of coherence, in fact, almost the maximum degree possible. Given that the unplanned passages operated far below this level, it would seem that such a high level of coherence requires special planning in the construction of a discourse segment around a given root metaphor and is not the default strategy that producers of discourse naturally and unconsciously adopt.

The following translation of one example is typical of our sample of the unplanned type of discourse (the metaphorical expressions are italicized, and the root metaphors appear in italicized capital letters and parentheses):

> Before *landing* (*POLITICS IS A JOURNEY*) in the Labor party he had *flirted* (*POLITICS IS ROMANTIC RELATIONS*) with the Likud party; nevertheless, his *roots* (*POLITICIANS ARE PLANTS*) have always been in the Labor party ideology.

Another interesting finding was that metaphorical shifts in the unplanned passages occurred not only at the intersentential level but also at the intrasentential level, that is, within the boundaries of the sentence unit. In other words, metaphorical shifts were found even at the clausal level. The following examples (taken from a different sample) illustrate these kinds of shifts:

> The peace process is *moving forward* and *ripening* (*FOREIGN POLICY IS A JOURNEY/FRUIT*).

> The first *step* [of the Oslo agreement], the real *embryonic* one, actually *works well* (*FOREIGN POLICY IS A JOURNEY/A PERSON/A MACHINE*).

> Violence is *eating away* the *foundations* of democracy (*THE POLITICAL SYSTEM IS A FOOD/A BUILDING*).

## Analysis 2: Global Coherence

Global coherence represents the homogeneity of the discourse in question, as measured by the ratio between the number of root metaphors instantiated in a passage and the total number of metaphorical expressions it contains. The reason such an additional analysis is needed is that linear coherence measures only sequential step-by-step shifts, but only a global coherence measure is sensitive to the total number of root metaphors that have been used throughout the passage. This measure represents another aspect of the metaphorical coherence of a discourse.

Basically, the least coherent discourse would be one in which the number of root metaphors equals the number of metaphorical expressions, yielding a score of 1; the higher the score, that is, the higher the number of metaphorical expressions that cluster under a smaller number of root metaphors, the higher the global coherence of the passage.

Using a $t$ test for unpaired variables, we found a significant difference in global coherence between the planned and unplanned passages, $p < .001$. Planned passages ($M = 6.77$, $SD = 5.12$) exhibited a much higher level than unplanned passages ($M = 1.42$, $SD = 0.24$). In other words, the ratio between the number of metaphorical expressions in a passage divided by the number of root metaphors they represented was much higher for the planned passages than for the unplanned ones.

## Analysis 3: Global Coherence and Conventionality

Although the global coherence of the planned passages was much higher than that of the unplanned ones, this analysis did not distinguish between conventional and novel expressions. We were interested in finding out to what extent the use of the underlying root metaphors in the planned passages supported the use of consistent conventional expressions. Recall that the linguistic assumption maintains that the use of a certain conventional expression reflects the use of the corresponding root metaphor. This should also work in the opposite direction; that is, when the root metaphor is being used, it should support the use of corresponding conventional expressions. If this is correct, we would expect to find that intensive use of a certain root metaphor also supports the use of clusters of the conventional metaphorical expressions that, according to the CM view, tend to cluster together.

We thus conducted the following analysis: First, we extracted all the clusters (either conventional or novel instantiations, or both) of consistent metaphorical expressions. Each cluster contained at least three instantiations that belonged with the same root metaphor. We then calculated the percentage of conventional instantiations within each cluster.

The results were unequivocal: The percentage of conventional expressions within each cluster was, on average, 9.7%. That is, in practice the only clusters of consistent metaphorical expressions found in the planned passages consisted of novel expressions. Thus, even passages that clearly made use of certain root metaphors did not support the use of their corresponding conventional expressions.

### Analysis 4: Shifts and Alternative Expressions

The previous analysis showed a significant difference in the level of metaphorical coherence between the two text types. Note, however, that one potential objection to this analysis is that the predominance of metaphorical shifts in the unplanned discourse (as opposed to the planned type) might derive from the lack of available conventional expressions belonging to the same root metaphor, compelling the producer of the discourse to make use of instantiations of different root metaphors. For example, in a phrase such as "he cooked up a trap," which represents a shift from the domain of food to that of hunting, perhaps there is no conventional metaphorical expression from the domain of food corresponding in meaning to *trap,* so that the producer of the sentence had no alternative but to create a shift. Thus, the analysis should examine whether alternative expressions (which are equally conventional and represent the same meaning) were available to the discourse producer but were not used.

To examine if this is indeed the case, we conducted another analysis in which alternative conventional expressions were sought for each shift. The more alternatives we could identify, the stronger the case against the CM theory.

*Procedure of analysis.* The first step was to decide which root metaphors would serve as the basis for our analysis. We immediately encountered a serious problem with this task because all the randomly selected unplanned passages contained a very large number of root metaphors. According to Lakoff and Johnson (1980), all those root metaphors must have been functionally activated, so that theoretically we had to treat every root metaphor as a main metaphor in the passage. However, it seemed unreasonable to analyze each of these many root metaphors as potentially the main root metaphors for the entire passage. Consequently, we used two criteria for selecting the root metaphors to be analyzed. The first criteria was to select the first root metaphor to be instantiated. The second criteria involved the selection of any other root metaphor with at least two instantiations in the passage. The rationale behind this decision was that, if we accept the CM theory, then the first root metaphor instantiated, or one that is instantiated more than once, can logically be assumed to have been used deliberately.

Once we had selected root metaphors using this procedure, the judges tried to look for available alternative expressions in Hebrew. Naturally, we did not find an alternative for each shift, either because of lack of creativity on our part or because, in many cases, no such conventional alternative exists.

We then conducted two tests to ensure that the alternatives we identified were indeed appropriate for the original expressions, that is, that they were similar in meaning and equally conventional. For the first test, five judges graded (on a scale from 1 to 5) the extent to which the two expressions shared the same meaning. We discarded all alternatives that scored less than 3. For the second test, five different judges graded (on a scale from 1 to 5) the frequency of occurrence of each metaphorical expression in ordinary discourse. We selected only those alternatives that were rated as either more conventional or up to one-half point less conventional than the original expressions they replaced. The following are translations of alternatives that survived all the selection criteria (metaphorical expressions are italicized, and metaphorical alternatives are underlined):

He *cooked up* (alternative: set) a *trap*.

The peace process is *moving forward* and *ripening* (alternative: getting closer to its destination).

### Results

The results clearly indicate the existence of a relatively large number of potential appropriate alternatives that were not used. On average, we found 2.2 appropriate alternatives per passage (out of 10.4 metaphorical expressions). Moreover, two factors may have prevented us from identifying an even higher number. First, we restricted our search to only one or two root metaphors for each passage, and second, we might simply not have been creative enough to come up with more alternatives even where such alternatives do exist in the language.

## GENERAL DISCUSSION

The picture that emerges from this analysis regarding the metaphorical coherence hypothesis is clear: None of the analyses supports the claim that, as a default, unplanned discourse exhibits a coherent distribution of metaphorical expressions. Contrary to the metaphorical coherence principle (which is compatible with the CM view), we found that unplanned discourse displays a significantly lower level of both linear and global coherence than does planned discourse. The use of metaphors in unplanned discourse appears more like free, uncontrolled "navigation" between a large number of root metaphors than a consistent elaboration of any unifying root metaphors. Indeed, special planning seems to be required to make discourse metaphorically coherent.

Furthermore, contrary to the predictions derived from the linguistic hypothesis, our third analysis of the distribution of consistent conventional (as opposed to novel) metaphorical expressions revealed that they do not tend to cluster together in natural discourse. That is, no co-occurrence of more than two or three conventional expressions sharing the same root metaphor (out of a much larger set of conventional expressions available in the language) was found in the 30 passages we analyzed: The passages contained either many conventional expressions representing different root metaphors (generally the unplanned discourse) or a large number of consistent novel expressions (usually the planned discourse).

To the extent that metaphorical coherence (or lack of it) reflects the use of root metaphors at some point in the production of the discourse in question, we found no evidence supporting the linguistic hypothesis. Rather, the fact that conventional metaphorical instantiations of a given metaphor appear in a given discourse does not necessarily seem to reflect a corresponding activation (in the producer's mind) of the root metaphor. Perhaps this means that the use of conventional expressions in real discourse is autonomous in that, under such conditions of natural discourse production, they do not rely on the functional activation of the entire root metaphor and, in that sense, their meanings are divorced from the underlying conceptual metaphors posited by the CM theory. The conventional expressions we use in ordinary language may have acquired a conventional meaning of their own and do not necessarily rely on the activation of the complex mapping of what are assumed to be their corresponding root metaphors (see Glucksberg & Keysar, 1990; McGlone, 1996).

Admittedly, our analyses are not online production analyses and may even be flawed in that they ignore certain potential factors that might influence the use of metaphorical expressions in discourse and bias unplanned discourse toward a metaphorically noncoherent structure (e.g., online production factors, norms of writing, genre characteristics, etc.). Future research in these areas is needed to get a fuller picture of the role played by conceptual metaphors in discourse production.

We might conclude that, although the conceptual root metaphors may be the metaphors we "live by," the actual use of metaphorical expressions in authentic natural discourse does not necessarily indicate that they are employed in the generation of that discourse.

## REFERENCES

Allbritton, D. W., McKoon, G., & Gerrig, R. J. (1995). Metaphor-based schemas and text representations: Making connections through conceptual metaphors. *Journal of Experimental Psychology: Learning, Memory, and Cognition, 21,* 612–625.

Boronat, C. B., & Gentner, D. (1999). *Metaphors are (sometimes) processed as generative domain-mappings.* Manuscript in preparation.

Freeman, D. (1995). Catch[ing] the nearest way: *Macbeth* and cognitive metaphor. *Journal of Pragmatics, 24,* 689–708.

Gentner, D., & Boronat, C. B. (1992, May). *Metaphor as mapping.* Paper presented at the Workshop on Metaphor, Tel Aviv University, Tel Aviv, Israel.

Gibbs, R. W. (1994). *The poetics of mind.* Cambridge, England: Cambridge University Press.

Glucksberg, S., & Keysar, B. (1990). Understanding metaphorical comparisons: Beyond similarity. *Psychological Review, 97,* 3–18.

Glucksberg, S., & McGlone, M. S. (in press). When love is not a journey: What metaphors mean. *Journal of Pragmatics.*

Kemper, S. (1989). Priming the comprehension of metaphors. *Metaphor and Symbolic Activity, 4,* 1–17.

Keysar, B., Shen, Y., & Glucksberg, S. (1998). *Conventional language: How metaphorical is it?* Manuscript submitted for publication.

Kreuz, R., & Graesser, A. (1991). Aspects of idiom interpretation: Comment on Nayak and Gibbs. *Journal of Experimental Psychology: General, 120,* 90–92.

Lakoff, G., & Johnson, M. (1980). *Metaphors we live by.* Chicago: University of Chicago Press.

Lakoff, G., & Turner, M. (1989). *More than cool reason: The power of poetic metaphor.* Berkeley: University of California Press.

McGlone, M. S. (1996). Conceptual metaphors and figurative language interpretation: Food for thought? *Journal of Memory and Language, 35,* 544–565.

Nayak, N. P., & Gibbs, R. (1990). Conceptual knowledge in the interpretation of idioms. *Journal of Experimental Psychology: General, 119,* 315–330.

# Readers as Text Processors and Performers: A New Formula for Poetic Intonation

Tom Barney
*Department of Linguistics and Modern English Language*
*Lancaster University*
*Lancaster, England*

Byers (1979) associates a number of characteristics with the intonation of recited verse, for example, slow speech rate, short tone units, narrow pitch range, and falling pitch patterns. Yet, whereas some of these features can be associated with verse recitation in particular, others occur elsewhere, for example, in liturgy and broadcasting, which suggests that they are intonational features not of verse recitation alone but of all vocal performance. In this article, a commercial recording of poetry is compared with a radio news broadcast to establish which prosodic features these two genres have in common and which are peculiar to poetry reading; the former are ascribed to a general "performance style," and the latter to poetic intonation proper. The question of which communicative and textual needs give rise to these features is discussed. In this way, a new and more refined "formula for poetic intonation" is established.

## PITCH PATTERNS AND THE STUDY OF VERSE PROSODY

Compared with studies of meter and rhythm, studies of the intonation of recited verse are fairly uncommon. Steele (1775/1969) argued for the importance of pitch patterns both in ordinary speech and in verse recitation. Steele's book was written to refute a previous claim by James Burnet, Lord Monboddo, in his *Of the Origin and Progress of Language* (1773–1792/1967), that the accentuation of English syllables was achieved only by an increase in loudness and not by any change in pitch. Steele argued that, on the contrary, "the melody of speech moves rapidly up and down by slides, wherein no graduated distinction of tones or semitones can be measured by the ear" (p. 4). Steele eventually convinced

---

Correspondence and requests for reprints should be sent to Tom Barney, Department of Linguistics and Modern English Language, Lancaster University, Bailrigg, Lancaster, LA1 4YT, United Kingdom. E-mail: T.Barney@lancaster.ac.uk

Monboddo of the existence of pitch melody in English speech. However, even though Steele had the better of the argument and he paid some attention to verse, most subsequent analysts of verse prosody have concentrated on the rhythmical beat to the exclusion of pitch patterns—on melody to the exclusion of measure.

The exceptions to this rule have not, on the whole, advanced our knowledge very far. One strand of thought has attempted to use intonation as a means of disambiguating verse (e.g., Brazil, 1992; Cauldwell, 1994; Cauldwell & Schourup, 1988; Chatman, 1956, 1966; Funkhouser, 1979; Loesch, 1965, 1966). The claim is that, if the words of a poem do not convey an unambiguous meaning, the way they are recited can. The problem with studies of this type tends to be that they assume more definite fixed meanings for intonation patterns than actually exist; intonational meaning is, in fact, far more beset with ambiguity than is verbal meaning, and thus, intonation does not provide the resource these authors clearly hoped it would.

A more productive strand of work has attempted to identify the intonational features that are specific to verse recitation as well as the features of poetic texts that give rise to their use. Some of this work has examined the way intonation patterns function as an exponent of verse form and line structure, showing that there is a tension between the variable structure of intonation and the fixed patterns of meter and that intonation is what gives prosodic form to free verse, where there is no meter (e.g., Crystal, 1975; Mukařovský, 1933; Taglicht, 1971). Others have looked at the kinds of patterns that are particularly associated with verse recitation (e.g., Byers, 1979, 1980, 1983; Wichmann, 1987). More recently, Tsur (1997a, 1997b, 1997c) used computer technology to make extremely detailed examinations of pitch movements and other features at the subsyllabic level.

## THIS STUDY

This study is an attempt to reexamine the notion of *poetic intonation* as a special variety of prosody. I take for granted that such a variety exists but question the assumption that it can be defined simply as the intonational features that are found in poetic recitation. These, taken together, by definition constitute *poetic recitation style,* but it does not follow that they cannot be found in any other stylistic variant of prosody. The problem is to decide which of them are unique to poetic recitation and which, occurring elsewhere, are not in themselves characteristic of poetry as such.

My starting point is the formula for poetic intonation given by Byers (1979). She analyzed recordings of six speakers reading both poetic and nonpoetic texts, drawing up from her findings a list "of the intonational qualities particularly characteristic of poetry" that "will constitute a rudimentary formula for poetic intonation":

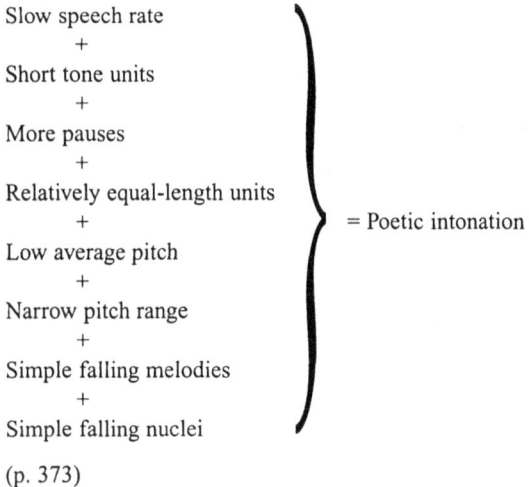

(p. 373)

The problem with this formula is that, although these may all be characteristics of poetic intonation, some of them are also associated with other varieties of nonspontaneous speech. This is true of slow speech rate, for example. Bolinger (1989) talked of "a sort of 'reading stereotype' " (p. 68) of falling pitch melodies, a stereotype that applies to all kinds of reading aloud. It appears, then, that some items in Byers's (1979) formula are really intonational characteristics of vocal performance in general, which distinguish it from spontaneous speech, and that their presence in the formula simply reflects the fact that poetic recitation is a form of vocal performance. On the other hand, short or relatively equal-length tone units are what we might expect to occur in poetic recitation because tone units in poetic recitation are recognized to be exponents of the verse line (e.g., Crystal, 1975), and verse is distinguished from other text types that are read aloud by its shorter and typically equal-length lines. It appears necessary, then, to refine the formula for poetic intonation to distinguish between features of poetic intonation proper and those of a general vocal-performance style. The study in this article is a first step in doing this.

What follows is a case study of two examples of nonspontaneous speech, a poetic recitation and a radio news broadcast. The poem is "Engineers' Corner," by Wendy Cope, read by the author.[1] Cope is a bestselling poet in Britain, with a reputation for light verse and parodies.

---

[1] The poem is from *Making Cocoa for Kingsley Amis* by Wendy Cope, 1986, London: Faber & Faber. Copyright 1986 by Wendy Cope. Reprinted by kind permission of Faber & Faber Ltd.

### Engineers' Corner

> Why isn't there an Engineers' Corner in Westminster Abbey? In Britain we've always made more fuss of a ballad than a blueprint ... How many schoolchildren dream of becoming great engineers?
>
> *Advertisement placed in* The Times *by the Engineering Council*

We make more fuss of ballads than of blueprints—  
That's why so many poets end up rich,  
While engineers scrape by in cheerless garrets.  
Who needs a bridge or dam? Who needs a ditch?  

Whereas the person who can write a sonnet          5  
Has got it made. It's always been the way,  
For everybody knows that we need poems  
And everybody reads them every day.  

Yes, life is hard if you choose engineering—  
You're sure to need another job as well;          10  
You'll have to plan your projects in the evenings  
Instead of going out. It must be hell.  

While well-heeled poets ride around in Daimlers,  
You'll burn the midnight oil to earn a crust,  
With no hope of a statue in the Abbey,          15  
With no hope, even, of a modest bust.  

No wonder small boys dream of writing couplets  
And spurn the bike, the lorry and the train.  
There's far too much encouragement for poets—  
That's why this country's going down the drain.          20  

The broadcast was the first 60 s of the news on BBC Radio 3 at 8 a.m. on Monday, July 6, 1998. Radio 3 is one of five national BBC radio stations; it deals mainly in classical music and erudite talks. It has a subacademic style, disliked by some, revered by others; this style carries over into the news bulletins. The transcript following is shown without punctuation:

BBC Radio 3 news, 8 a.m., Monday 6 July 1998

hundreds of orangemen have spent the night camped in the  
fields around Drumcree parish church in their stand off with the security forces  
the troops are preventing them from entering the mainly nationalist Garvaghy  
road the route of their annual parade there was some violence across the  
province last night as loyalists angry at the ban on the march blockaded some  
roads and set fire to cars  

the government is announcing proposals to change the way the Child Support  
Agency operates one plan is expected to include a simpler formula for assessing  
maintenance payments

doctors holding their annual conference in Cardiff will today discuss the government's pledge to cut hospital waiting lists the BMA will warn ministers not to shorten waiting lists at the expense of maintaining hospitals and equipment

the government has asked the European Commission to investigate why many cars cost more in Britain than on the rest of the continent tonight's Panorama programme will produce evidence that Mercedes Volkswagen and Volvo operate price fixing in breach of E.U. competition regulations the manufacturers claim that the price difference is due to the strong pound

I compared these two texts for the incidence of each of the features identified by Byers (1979). The idea is that this detailed study of two texts goes beyond Byers's formula by dividing the intonational features given in that formula into those that can be found in both texts, which are therefore more likely to be general performance style features, and those found wholly or mainly in the poem, which are more likely to be poetic features proper. This gives a revised formula for poetic intonation that can then be further refined through studies of larger corpora of nonspontaneous speech that contain many more examples of these and other text types.

### Slow Speech Rate

It is immediately clear that Cope reads her poem more slowly than the Radio 3 news is read. There is, however, an important qualification. Cope prefaces the poem with a short explanation of how it came to be written, in the course of which she reads out her epigraph (the advertisement from *The Times*). She speaks faster in this preface than in her reading of the poem except when she is quoting the advertisement. Here she slows down and introduces some glottal stops at the beginnings of words, a feature also clearly audible in the poem. Because the quotation from the advertisement is nonspontaneous, being read from a text, it would appear that a slow speech rate is part of Cope's performance style, whether or not it is poetry she is performing. Moreover, I have an impression, as a regular Radio 3 listener, that the newsreader in our extract, Paul Guinery, is a faster reader than is usual on the station. In short, we cannot be sure, based on the evidence before us, that slow speech rate is a characteristic of poetic intonation in our narrower definition; by default, we must assume that it is a feature of general performance style.

### Tone Unit Length

The tone unit "chunks" speech into audible segments. It has been defined as "an intuitively perceived tone-cum-rhythm unit" (Trim, 1959/1973, p. 321). A unit of this kind, which hangs together both rhythmically and as a pitch melody, has been used by most British analysts of intonation. I have found, however, that pitch and rhythmic groups are frequently independent of each other (Barney, 1998) and have therefore divided them into distinct groups, as American analysts have tend-ed to do (e.g., Pike, 1945). The *nucleus group* I define rhythmically: It consists essentially of a stretch of speech from an initial accent, the *onset,* through a trajectory to a final accent, the *nucleus,* which is typically some kind of drawn-out pitch movement or glide (see Crystal, 1969, pp. 207–208). The *tune* is a pitch melody, a perceptible single pitch contour. A tune may contain one or more nucleus groups.

Table 1 shows how the two texts compare for the length of prosodic groups, measuring length by the number of syllables that groups contain; that is, it shows how many groups in each text contain what number of syllables. The average group lengths are shorter for Cope than for Radio 3, especially for nucleus groups; her maximum group length is also shorter. The distribution of groups of different lengths shows that, for Cope, groups cluster more closely around the average length than they do for Radio 3; Cope's prosodic groups are, in fact, more equal in length. Shorter and more equal prosodic groups do appear to be a feature of poetic intonation in the narrow sense. The reason for this is clear. For Cope, the maximum group length is 11 syllables: The length of an iambic pentameter line with a feminine ending, as shown in Figure 1. (In all figures, the symbol / over a syllable indicates that the syllable carries a pitch accent; the symbol ' indicates that the syllable is prominent but unaccented.) Eleven of 20 lines are rendered with a single tune like this. Moreover, 7 of the other 9 lines are rendered with two tunes, with the division between them coming in a syntactically convenient place midline, congruent with the traditional notion of the caesura, as shown in Figure 2 (the vertical bar | indicates the tune boundary). An additional 4 lines that are not divided into two tunes are divided into two nucleus groups in similar fashion. In short, it is clear that the relatively short and equal-length prosodic groups in the poem are dictated by the formal textual

TABLE 1
Length of Prosodic Groups

| | | | | | | | | | | | | | |
|---|---|---|---|---|---|---|---|---|---|---|---|---|---|
| Cope (210 syllables) | | | | | | | | | | | | | |
| 31 tunes; average length of tunes = 7 syllables | | | | | | | | | | | | | |
| No. of syllables | 2 | 3 | 4 | 5 | 6 | 7 | 8 | 9 | 10 | 11 | | | |
| No. of tunes | 1 | 4 | 6 | 2 | 3 | 4 | 0 | 0 | 4 | 7 | | | |
| 51 nucleus (rhythmic) groups; average length of groups = 4 syllables | | | | | | | | | | | | | |
| No. of syllables | 1 | 2 | 3 | 4 | 5 | 6 | 7 | 8 | 9 | 10 | 11 | | |
| No. of groups | 2 | 11 | 9 | 10 | 7 | 5 | 5 | 1 | 0 | 0 | 1 | | |
| Radio 3 (306 syllables) | | | | | | | | | | | | | |
| 37 tunes; average length of tunes = 8 syllables | | | | | | | | | | | | | |
| No. of syllables | 2 | 3 | 4 | 5 | 6 | 7 | 8 | 9 | 10 | 11 | | | |
| No. of tunes | 1 | 1 | 3 | 5 | 5 | 4 | 4 | 5 | 1 | 0 | | | |
| No. of syllables | 12 | 13 | 14 | 15 | 16 | 17 | 18 | 19 | 20 | 21 | | | |
| No. of tunes | 1 | 3 | 1 | 0 | 0 | 1 | 0 | 0 | 1 | 1 | | | |
| 48 nucleus groups; average length of groups = 6 syllables | | | | | | | | | | | | | |
| No. of syllables | 2 | 3 | 4 | 5 | 6 | 7 | 8 | 9 | 10 | 11 | 12 | 13 | 14 |
| No. of groups | 4 | 1 | 9 | 8 | 5 | 6 | 5 | 3 | 3 | 1 | 1 | 1 | 1 |

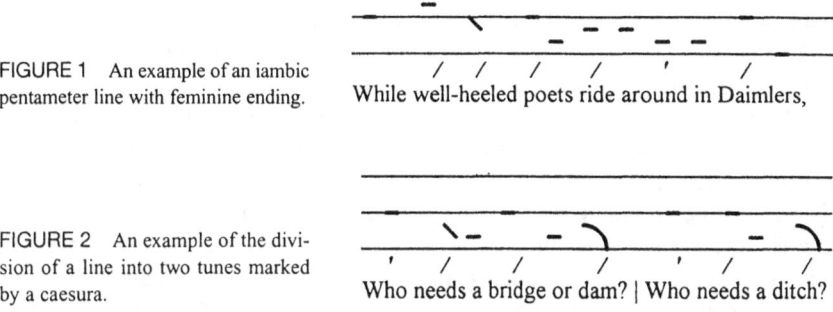

FIGURE 1  An example of an iambic pentameter line with feminine ending.

FIGURE 2  An example of the division of a line into two tunes marked by a caesura.

structure, which is unique to verse texts. Group length in the Radio 3 extract is more variable, as Figure 3 shows.

## Pauses

In assessing the number of pauses in each reading, we must distinguish between actual momentary silences in the stream of speech, and the lengthening of syllables immediately before a point when a speaker wishes to indicate a discontinuity. Lengthening can accompany a silence but can also substitute for one (Knowles, 1991, p. 152). I reserve the term *pause* for an actual silence and, following Knowles, refer generically to pauses and final lengthening as *temporal discontinuity*. Because final lengthening can substitute for pause (although it is presumably less emphatic), we must consider both phenomena when assessing Byers's (1979) claim that poetic recitation contains more pauses than other forms of speech.

We find that, in a text of 165 words, Cope has 40 temporal discontinuities, consisting of 32 pauses, and 8 cases of final lengthening alone; whereas the Radio 3 broadcast, in a text of 185 words, has 34 temporal discontinuities, consisting of 30 pauses, and 4 cases of final lengthening alone. Byers's (1979) inclusion of "more pauses" in her formula for poetic intonation seems justified.

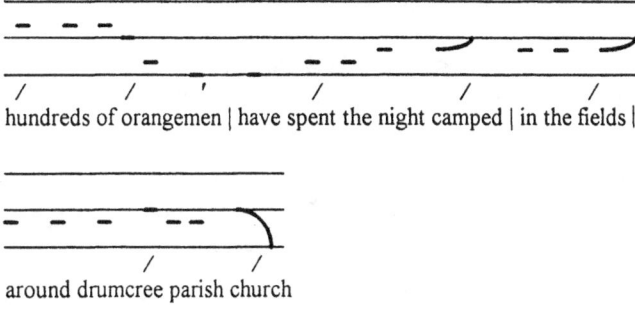

FIGURE 3  An example of variable group length in the Radio 3 extract.

For Cope, the places in which these discontinuities occur include all 19 line boundaries, of which only the end of line 2 is marked by final lengthening alone, and 18 caesuras (i.e., midline sentence, clause, or phrase boundaries), of which only three cases are marked by final lengthening alone. The remaining two temporal discontinuities are after *Yes* (line 9) and *You'll* (line 14), which are apparently done for emphasis: a pause for effect, in this case, an ironic effect. In general, however, temporal discontinuities are, like prosodic groups, exponents of the verse structure, marking the ends of lines and half lines. This reinforces the raw figures in suggesting that a high incidence of temporal discontinuities is a feature of poetic intonation rather than simply of performance intonation.

If we now examine the Radio 3 extract, we find a tendency to agglutinate prosodic groups, that is, to omit temporal discontinuities at the ends of groups, where we might expect them. The example in Figure 4 contains three nucleus groups but no temporal discontinuities. There is, however, one context in which "too many" pauses do occur. This happens toward the end of the second and fourth news items. These pauses are of the kind Abercrombie (1971/1991) called *silent stress*. Here the pauses fulfill what he called the *terminal function* of silent stress: They indicate that the end of something is approaching, and they do this by occurring in syntactically and semantically unpredictable places, often very frequently. For example (the vertical bars here indicate the pauses):

one plan is expected to include | a simpler formula | for assessing | maintenance payments

According to Abercrombie, terminal silent stresses are found especially in broadcasting. It appears, then, that these momentary increases in the frequency of pauses do not suggest that more pauses are, after all, a feature of general performance style; silent stresses are a feature of broadcasting style, which, like poetic recitation, is a special case of performance style.

## Pitch and Pitch Range

I divide pitch into five levels: (a) top (the upper extremity of a speaker's range), (b) high (between top and the midline), (c) the midline itself, (d) low (between the midline and the lower extremity), and (e) base (the lower extremity itself). Table 2 shows for each reading how many syllables were spoken at each level.

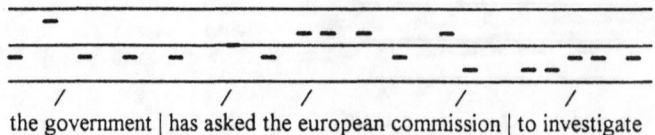

FIGURE 4  An example of three nucleus groups but no temporal discontinuities.

TABLE 2
Number of Syllables at Each Pitch Level

|  | Pitch Levels | | |
| --- | --- | --- | --- |
|  | Top/High | Low/Base | Mid |
| Cope | 11 | 174 | 50 |
| Radio 3 | 16 | 280 | 27 |

Obviously, for both readings, going above the midline is an occasional device only. Both readings, then, have what Byers (1979) predicted for poetic intonation: low average pitch and narrow pitch range. What occasions serve to cue a venture above the midline? In some cases, two or more syllables that do this occur in the same word or phrase, so they can be regarded as part of a single vocal gesture. Consolidating these, we find that Cope moves above the midline eight times, namely, *make* (line 1), *That's* (line 2), *person* (line 5), *have to* (line 11), *well* (line 13), *No* (line 17), *far too* (line 19), and *That's* (line 20). These include four of five stanza openings; the remainder are all line openings. The Radio 3 extract moves above the midline six times: *hundreds of, violence, government is announcing proposals, doctors, government has asked the European Commission,* and *many*. These include the openings of all four news stories and the shift of focus in the first item ("there was some violence . . .") from Drumcree in particular to the whole of Northern Ireland. So, in the reading of both text types, the use of high pitch is a means of indicating initiation, with both having a general prevalence of low and narrow pitch. In fact, these features are not confined to poetic intonation; on the contrary the Radio 3 extract has the narrower range. Pitch rises less often than in the Cope poem even as far as the midline, whereas if we examine pitch movements, we find that the Radio 3 extract has a much higher proportion of syllables that repeat the pitch of their predecessor (78.9% vs. 23.7% for Cope) rather than move up or down from it. The poem's wider pitch range suggests that, as we might expect, the recitation of poetry is associated with more prototypically dramatic effects than is newsreading. (I have an impression that, when professional actors recite poetry, they tend to use a wider pitch range than do poets or the academics and students I used in my doctoral research.[2])

### Falling Melodies and Falling Nuclei

The *nucleus* is the last—and is traditionally considered to be the most prominent—pitch accent in a pitch contour. The type of pitch movement made on the nucleus has very often been used to classify the entire pitch contour in which a

---

[2]I am grateful to Reuven Tsur, who in this connection observed to me that John Gielgud, in his readings of Shakespeare's sonnets, uses an exceptionally wide pitch range.

nucleus occurs (e.g., Crystal, 1969). Byers (1979), however, made a distinction between falling nuclei and falling *melodies* (i.e., pitch contours as a whole).

If we examine our data for the prevalence of falling melodies and falling nuclei we find that, with one exception, Cope uses nothing but falling melodies and falling nuclei throughout her recitation. For example, line 12 (Figure 5) consists of two tunes, both of which maintain a downward trend of pitch throughout their length, and both of which end with downglides on the nuclei, on *out* and *hell*. The exception to this pattern is line 5 (Figure 6). Here there is a rise in pitch on the last syllable of *sonnet*. This, however, is a very small exception: The trend of pitch is downward throughout most of the contour—it is, generally speaking, a falling melody—and the upglide when it comes is a very small one. The contour still ends at a low pitch.

With the Radio 3 extract, we have more variety of pitch patterns. There are 11 tunes with end rises, and 3 more which, although they end in falls, have a rising trend throughout their length until the end fall. However, when taken together, these patterns still constitute fewer than half of the 37 tunes in this extract. End-rising tunes are used to indicate incompletion—that more material related to what has just been said follows. When the segment of text that completes such a sequence is delivered, an end-falling tune is normally used. If we return to the example in Figure 3, we see that the tunes on *have spent the night camped* and *in the fields* both rise in pitch throughout, whereas the final tune, on *around Drumcree parish church,* falls from about halfway through and ends with a downglide. When a tune is used that rises most of the way but ends with a fall, this flags a topic shift (Figure 7). In this example, the Child Support Agency is the topic of the news item but is not mentioned right at the beginning of the item; when it is mentioned, this is marked by the unusual pitch pattern.

The difference between the two text types in the degree of predominance of falling tunes and nuclei is something of a surprise; in view of Bolinger's (1989) remark, quoted earlier, about a "reading stereotype," we would expect falling pitch patterns to be a performance and not a poetic feature. This, however, is a matter of degree. In the Radio 3 extract, falling patterns still predominate—very nearly 60% of the tunes are simple falling melodies. Although the evidence is somewhat equiv-

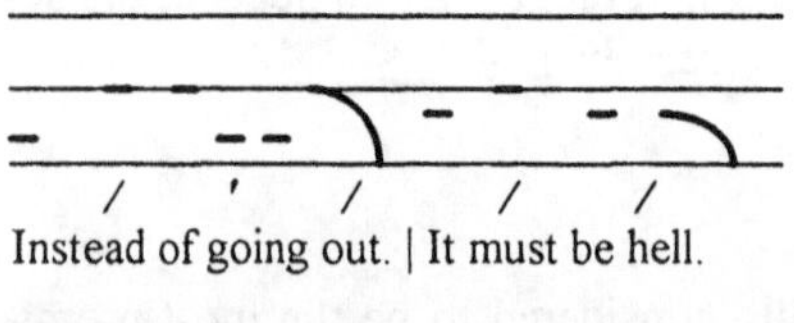

FIGURE 5  An explication of line 12 of Cope's poem.

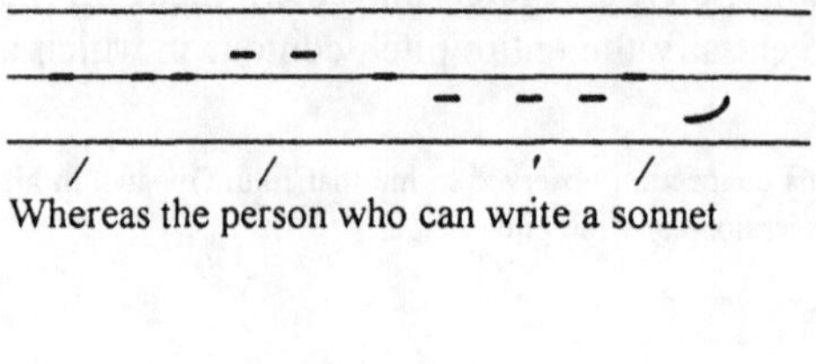

FIGURE 6  An explication of line 5 of Cope's poem.

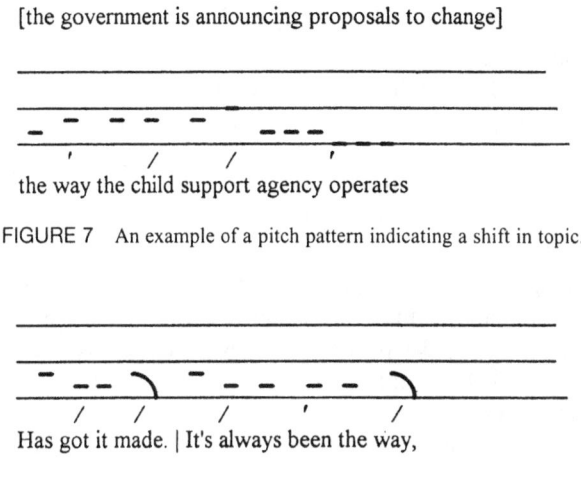

FIGURE 7  An example of a pitch pattern indicating a shift in topic.

FIGURE 8  An explication of line 6 of Cope's poem.

ocal, it does suggest that falling pitch patterns may be a feature of general performance style but that poetic intonation may make greater use of it.

### Echoes

One feature of poetic intonation that Byers (1979) did not mention is a tendency for pitch patterns to repeat themselves exactly as a way of binding together segments of text that are in close proximity or that are parallel in some way. For example, Cope reads line 6 of the poem as shown in Figure 8. The two tunes used here both have a drop in pitch immediately after the first syllable, followed by a level stretch at the lower pitch, then a reset to the initiation point of a final downglide. This echo joins together the two halves of the line and emphasizes the presence of the caesura. Echo occurs only very occasionally in the Radio 3 extract; what we find there, rather, are broad similarities between pitch patterns, for example, between general trends over whole contours, combined with differences of detail. One clear feature of poetic intonation is its stylization, reflecting the stylization of verse as a graphological form.

### A NEW FORMULA FOR POETIC INTONATION

We can summarize our findings in the form of a tentative new formula for poetic intonation, which gives a set of intonational characteristics of poetry recitation but distinguishes among those that are part of poetic intonation proper, those that are part of general performance style, and those that fall between:

| Performance Features | Specifically Poetic Features |
|---|---|
| Slow speech rate | Short tone units |
| Low average pitch | More pauses |
| Narrow pitch range | Relatively equal-length units |
| | Echoes between pitch patterns |
| | Simple falling melodies |
| | Simple falling nuclei |

It is worth emphasizing that the specifically poetic features are exponents of the formal prosodic structure of the verse, in particular its division into lines and half lines. That this association can be made lends weight to the view that these are indeed features specifically of poetic recitation and not merely ones that happen to occur in this recitation.

This formula as we have it leaves much out. We need to know, for example, whether the poetic features are found across a wide range of verse styles, how far different verse-speaking styles exist, and whether the general performance features can be found in nonspontaneous speech other than poetry recitation and radio news broadcasts. In this article, I have provided the beginnings of a model of poetic intonation, which, rather than being a simple list of features, has begun the task of ascribing the features of poetic intonation to specific aspects of text and performance. I hope this preliminary work will serve as a hypothesis to be tested and refined through a comprehensive version of such a model.

## REFERENCES

Abercrombie, D. (1991). Some functions of silent stress. In *Fifty years in phonetics* (pp. 71–80). Edinburgh, Scotland: Edinburgh University Press. (Original work published 1971)

Barney, T. (1998). *Style in performance: The prosody of poetic recitation.* Unpublished doctoral dissertation, University of Lancaster, Lancaster, England.

Bolinger, D. (1989). *Intonation and its uses.* London: Edward Arnold.

Brazil, D. (1992). Listening to people reading. In M. Coulthard (Ed.), *Advances in spoken discourse analysis* (pp. 209–241). London: Routledge.

Burnet, J., Lord Monboddo (1967). *Of the origin and progress of language.* Menston, England: Scolar Press. (Original work published 1773–1792)

Byers, P. B. (1979). A formula for poetic intonation. *Poetics, 8,* 367–380.

Byers, P. B. (1980). Intonation prediction and the sound of poetry. *Language and Style, 13,* 3–14.

Byers, P. B. (1983). The auditory reality of the verse line. *Style, 17,* 27–36.

Cauldwell, R. (1994). *Discourse intonation and recordings of poetry: Philip Larkin reads "Mr Bleaney."* Unpublished doctoral dissertation, University of Birmingham, Birmingham, England.

Cauldwell, R., & Schourup, L. (1988). Discourse intonation and recordings of poetry: A study of Yeats's readings. *Language and Style, 21,* 411–426.

Chatman, S. (1956). Robert Frost's "Mowing": An inquiry into prosodic structure. *Kenyon Review, 18,* 421–428.

Chatman, S. (1966). On the intonational fallacy. *Quarterly Journal of Speech, 52,* 283–286.

Crystal, D. (1969). *Prosodic systems and intonation in English.* Cambridge, England: Cambridge University Press.

Crystal, D. (1975). Intonation and metrical theory. In *The English tone of voice* (pp. 105–124). London: Edward Arnold.
Funkhouser, L. B. (1979). Acoustic rhythm in Randall Jarrell's *The death of the ball turret gunner. Poetics, 8,* 381–403.
Knowles, G. (1991). Prosodic labelling: The problem of tone group boundaries. In S. Johansson & A. B. Stenstrom (Eds.), *English computer corpora: Selected papers and research guide* (pp. 149–163). Amsterdam: Mouton de Gruyter.
Loesch, K. T. (1965). Literary ambiguity and oral performance. *Quarterly Journal of Speech, 51,* 258–267.
Loesch, K. T. (1966). A reply to Mr. Chatman. *Quarterly Journal of Speech, 52,* 286–289.
Mukařovský, J. (1933). Intonation comme facteur de rhythme poetique [Intonation as an element of poetic rhythm]. *Archives Neerlandaises de phonetique experimentale, 8–9,* 153–165.
Pike, K. L. (1945). *The intonation of American English.* Ann Arbor: University of Michigan Press.
Steele, J. (1969). *An essay towards establishing the melody and measure of speech.* Menston, England: Scolar Press. (Original work published 1775)
Taglicht, J. (1971). The function of intonation in English verse. *Language and Style, 4,* 116–122.
Trim, J. L. M. (1973). Major and minor tone-groups in English. In W. E. Jones & J. Laver (Eds.), *Phonetics in linguistics: A book of readings* (pp. 320–323). London: Longman. (Original work published 1959)
Tsur, R. (1997a). Douglas Hodge reading Keats's Elgin Marbles sonnet. *Style, 31,* 34–57.
Tsur, R. (1997b). Sound affects of poetry: Critical impressionism, reductionism and cognitive poetics. *Pragmatics and Cognition, 5,* 283–304.
Tsur, R. (1997c). "To be or not to be"—That is the rhythm: A cognitive–empirical study of poetry in the theatre. *Assaph C, 13,* 95–122.
Wichmann, A. (1987). *Stylistic variation in prosody: A preliminary study of the Spoken English Corpus.* Unpublished master's dissertation, Lancaster University, Lancaster, England.

# Spotlight on Spectators: Emotions in the Theater

## Elly A. Konijn
*Faculty of Arts*
*Vrije Universiteit*

In investigating theater spectators and their aesthetic experiences, a sociological and a psychological orientation on contemporary theater research were compared. Field studies usually concern sociological variables (e.g., age, education, and appreciation). If occasionally the spectator's emotional experience is explored, the Aristotelian viewpoint prevails, resulting in the identification hypothesis. This study opts for a broader perspective based on contemporary emotion psychology. Over 350 spectators completed a questionnaire that represented viewpoints from sociological, psychological, and theater studies perspectives. High-status audiences found the selected performances neither complex nor unconventional and hardly experienced identification emotions but rather experienced empathy and positive task emotions. Their overall appreciation referred mainly to the actor's performance, which was also the strongest source for spectators' emotions in the theater.

Two main perspectives can be distinguished in contemporary theater research that deal with real spectators in empirical field studies: a sociologically and a psychologically oriented perspective. Broadly speaking, research questions refer to what kinds of spectators watch what types of performances, what the reward is that theater spectators are looking for, and in what kinds of performances they expect to find it.

In short, the *sociological paradigm* states that art increases status and that spectators try to acquire it by visiting performances that are chic and in vogue with their own social group (Bourdieu, 1979; Ganzeboom & Ranshuysen, 1994; Knulst, 1989). In addition, recent scholars hold the position that complex and unconventional plays are considered more beautiful than other kinds by high-expert audiences. Such spectators would prefer art that demands a high level of information processing and takes place in an unconventional setting, that is, modern and not conservative (Berlyne, 1974; Ganzeboom, 1989; Maas, Verhoeff, & Ganzeboom 1990; Scitovsky, 1976). It is a cognitive approach to aesthetic experiences.

---

Correspondence and requests for reprints should be sent to Elly A. Konijn, *Vrije* Universiteit, Faculty of Arts, Sections General and Comparative Literature and Word and Image, De Boelelaan 1105, 1081 HV, Amsterdam, The Netherlands. E-mail: elly.konijn@let.uu.nl

The *psychological paradigm* of theater research is concerned with the affective benefits of attending performances. With its background in literature and art studies, the *Aristotelian paradigm* prevailed for a long period. In brief, it claims that spectators look for catharsis and identification in art that is familiar, compelling, and that evokes pity and fear (Aristotle, trans. 1968; see Kreitler & Kreitler, 1972; Schoenmakers, 1988, 1990, pp. 93–106). Concerning spectators' experiences, a recently developed paradigm is based on (emotion) psychology from the 1980s and 1990s. Briefly, it posits that spectators want to understand and to feel in order to satisfy their concerns and needs and that they do so by visiting plays that are interesting, exciting, and moving (Greenberg, 1976; McGuire, 1974; Tan, 1996; Zillmann, 1991).

To understand the aesthetic experiences of theater spectators, I summarize and integrate the main variables of the sociological, psychological, and theater studies perspectives. Assumptions and hypotheses from the different perspectives were empirically tested on the same sample. The hypotheses can be briefly stated as the *high-status hypothesis,* the *complexity–conventionality hypothesis,* the *identification hypothesis,* and the *emotion hypothesis.* The hypotheses are elaborated in subsequent sections. Results are discussed with regard to their contribution to the spectators' appreciation of the performances.

## PERSPECTIVES ON SPECTATORS: WHO IS LOOKING FOR WHAT?

### The Sociological Perspective and Its Hypotheses

Within the sociological paradigm, sociographic variables such as age, sex, education, and income are thought to explain differences in choices and appreciation for various cultural products. Following Bourdieu (1979), art consumption is seen as a tool for the cultural and economic elite to distinguish themselves from ordinary society, thus establishing their high status. They are attracted to art that is highly estimated among their own social group (i.e., peer grouping). The emphasis seems to be on the elite, whereas the "ordinary people" would mainly act to the contrary. High status is usually defined as high income or high educational level or both, and would account for most of the variance associated with the reception of cultural products (including performances). In modern society, however, the cultural elite may be poor and the financial elite may be poorly educated. Do the highly educated never have a good laugh at *The Benny Hill Show?* What about performances that are difficult to understand for the highly educated and simple for others, such as folklore? At its premiere in Paris, Samuel Beckett's *Waiting for Godot* was not understood by the regular theatergoer but was greatly admired by inhabitants of a prison (Esslin, 1961).

Society now seems to be dividing more and more into autonomous groups, without a status-based order of relationships: "Life style and taste are acquired increasingly by individuals themselves and seem to be less and less determined by the social group in which one is born" (Abbing, 1986, p. 98). Dijkstra (1992, pp. 230–233) emphasized that social approval and behavioral support within social networks of peer groups are more important for reading behavior than the presupposed increasing effect of status. These social networks can be considered segments of society based on lifestyles. In addition to sociological factors, Dijkstra underscored the more personal factors to explain reading behavior. In a broader sense, it seems important to study sociological variables in combination with psychological variables to explain cultural behavior (Abbing, 1986; Greenberg, 1976; McGuire, 1974; van Trijp, 1997). Ganzeboom (1989) and Maas et al. (1990) also admitted that a spectator visits the theater, for example, because it fulfills aesthetic pleasures apart from social-status drives and motives. However, these authors related aesthetic pleasure only to the spectator's capacity for information processing, which they link directly to educational level.

As an extension of Bourdieu's (1979) theory, Ganzeboom (1989) and Maas et al. (1990) emphasized the importance of specific product characteristics for art appreciation. Particular features of spectators (e.g., education) would relate to particular features of the cultural product to explain preferences. These product characteristics are conventionality, unconventionality, complexity, and noncomplexity. The dimension (un)conventionality refers to the setting of the performance (e.g., a traditional theater) and to the way the performance is designed (e.g., modern or experimental). *Conventional* art relies on common, accepted, traditional, and usually conservative attitudes and norms (Ganzeboom & Ranshuysen, 1994; Maas et al., 1990). On the contrary, *unconventional* art has an innovative, modern, experimental, and usually progressive character. Furthermore, Maas et al. related conventionality to a person's professional status. In-group norms of people with lower professions would focus on conventional and conservative art forms, whereas those of higher professions would focus on unconventional and progressive ones.

The complexity dimension refers to both semantic and formal features of the cultural product. *Complexity* refers to art that offers unexpected, unusual, and new information and, therefore, is not easy to understand, whereas *noncomplex* art offers simple, predictable, ordinary, and "known" information, which allows the spectator to more or less relax (Ganzeboom & Ranshuysen, 1994; Maas et al., 1990). Following Berlyne's (1970, 1974) hypothesis that a higher level of information processing increases aesthetic pleasure, Maas et al. argued that complexity relates to one's capacity for information processing. Berlyne as well as Scitovsky (1976) proposed that there is an optimum among complexity, arousal, and hedonic pleasure. In the views of Maas et al. and Ganzeboom and Ranshuysen, complexity also calls upon the intellectual capacities of spectators. Moreover, they relate information-processing capacity directly to educational level. In this view, aesthetic pleasure is understood in a rather restricted, that is, cognitive, sense. The affective component seems to be underestimated.

The hypotheses following the sociological perspective can be summarized as the high-status hypothesis and the complexity–conventionality hypothesis. That is, Ganzeboom and Ranshuysen (1994) relate unconventionality to Bourdieu's (1979) hypothesis that people strive for higher status and relate complexity to Berlyne's (1970) hypothesis that a higher level of information processing increases aesthetic pleasure. Furthermore, high-status spectators would appreciate complex and unconventional plays more than other kinds, in an unconventional setting—that is, modern and not conservative.

### The Psychological Perspective and Its Hypotheses

Emotional experiences are central to the arts, in production and in reception. Already in Aristotle's *Poetics* (trans. 1968), theatrical experiences are described in terms of "pity and fear" and at a more abstract level as "catharsis." Although the precise meaning of catharsis is much debated (see Schoenmakers, 1990, pp. 93–106, 1992), it clearly is related to emotional experiences during the reception process. The Aristotelian paradigm is quite common among literary scholars, in practically oriented art studies, and in lay theory. Concerning the experiences of spectators, it focuses mainly on traditional—whole—characters, with whom spectators supposedly identify ("I feel just like Hedda Gabler"). Because prototypical emotions are central to main characters (Konijn, 1994; Laffont, 1960; Polti, 1990), identification should mainly relate to these "big" emotions, such as love, hate, and anger. Prototypical emotions are among the first to be reported if participants are asked to name an emotion (Mesquita, 1993; cf. basic emotions in Ekman, 1982). Yet, why should spectators' emotions be limited to or even be focused on those few? And how many other emotions are also relevant?

The meaning of the term *identification* differs according to the particular art form, the specific field of research, the particular scholar, and is often confounded with the concept of empathy (for an overview, see Schoenmakers, 1988; Zillmann, 1991). Zillmann (1994) questioned the usefulness of the concept of identification "in explaining emotional reactivity to drama" (p. 33). Some empirical results (Schälzky, 1980; Westerbeek, 1995; Wildschut, 1995) do not support emotional parallelism between character and spectator. Studies using identification scales show conflicting and incomparable results or actually use a broader concept of *involvement* (Schmitz & Vorderer, 1998; Schoenmakers, 1986; Schram, 1985, pp. 180–245; van Vliet, 1991). The statements in these scales usually reflect some attitude toward character or play, and the content of the scale is often confounded with statements referring to empathy or general aspects of appraisal.

Another drawback of the identification hypothesis is its fixation on the fictional characters, although their importance as impetus of emotions is merely assumed. What about the soundtrack? What about the narrative or the situation? Contemporary emotion psychology teaches that emotions are evoked mainly by appraisals of particular features in the situation that are relevant to a person's concerns, drives, motives, and goals (Frijda, 1986). Likewise, in attributing emotions to a character (or persons in daily life), contextual information turns out to be crucial for emotion determination (Hess & Kleck, 1994; Konijn, 1994; Shields, 1984). Fictional characters are only one source of information. Moreover, modern fictional characters are often scattered or fragmented, making it hard to identify with them. The Aristotelian paradigm seems to neglect modern art forms as well as aesthetic experiences other than catharsis and identification.

Contemporary psychology ascribes a central role to emotions as important drives or motivating factors for human behavior (e.g., Frijda, 1986, 1988). Based on Frijda's (1986) emotion theory, Tan (1994, 1996, p. 79) theorized that spectators want maximal emotional benefit from watching movies. Zillmann (1994, p. 48) mentioned that emotions feed the spectator's evaluation and appreciation of cinema and theater. Schoenmakers' (1986) field study suggested that an increase in emotional intensity goes along with an increase in spectators' appreciation for the performance, even if they experienced negative emotions (e.g., sadness). The emotion paradigm that is promoted in this study adheres to a rather complex psychological theory of daily life emotions, which is still incoherent with regard to the theatrical experiences of spectators. Two views on spectators' emotions prevail here: Tan (1994, 1996) and Konijn (Hoorn & Konijn, 1999). Tan (1996, pp. 34–36) stated that emotions may result from sources or objects in the fiction (i.e., content) and from sources or objects in the artefact (i.e., form). Emotional appraisals referring to the fiction may be "Hedda Gabler has a disgusting character! But I am just like her" or "I feel pity for her sufferings." Emotions from the fiction can be identified as identification or empathy, but Tan favors empathy. Emotions elicited by the artefact are illustrated by "The soft tone of the light and the tender music makes me feel weak and enhances my pity." Thus, the same emotion word (*pity*) may have different objects (in fiction or in artefact).

This article emphasizes the specific emotions that result from the task of spectating, such as "I should concentrate better on the plot, but what a well-performed Hedda!" The understanding of the game that is played by the actors on stage (who often also play with the spectators) stirs task emotions in spectators. This idea parallels the task-emotion theory on acting by Konijn (1991, 1992, 1994, 1995, in press; Konijn & Westerbeek, 1997). These studies present empirical support that professional actors generally do not identify with the character in a performance: Their emotional experiences are not significantly correlated to the character emotions they express. While performing on stage, the professional actors mainly experience emotions of a different nature. These emotions are interpreted as a result of doing the job of acting, specifically, performing the acting tasks while many evaluative and critical eyes are watching (e.g., "I have to speak up with this audience," or "An important critic is among them").[1]

---

[1] I presume that actors can use their task emotions to shape character emotions on stage. To elaborate on this rather unusual statement is beyond the scope of this article. However, I would emphasize that the empirical support for the task-emotion theory in Konijn (1991, 1992, 1994, 1995, in press; Konijn & Westerbeek, 1997) is based on field studies with more than 300 professional actors randomly selected from The Netherlands, Flanders, and the United States.

In the same vein, spectators have their tasks while watching a performance, such as understanding the relationships between the characters and unraveling their motives. Thus, spectators may show task emotions of spectating, such as "I'm confused because I don't understand that story," or "I wonder, why that strange light?" More likely, task emotions of spectators will be of a positive nature, for instance, concentration, challenge, excitement, or admiration (for the actor's performance). It is expected that positive task emotions of spectators dominate over empathy and identification with the character.

Reiterating the objects of spectators' emotions, a third category may be added. Emotions may not only be triggered by objects in the fiction or artefact directly, as Tan (1996) proposed, they may also be fed by personal reminiscences and associations (e.g., "I cry, since Ophelia's death reminds me of my sister's suicide!"). Thus, indirectly, emotions may be evoked by what occurs on stage (e.g., "Her white dress reminds me of my mom's wedding gown") but may not be the actual object of emotion (e.g., "sister's suicide," or "mom's wedding gown"). Therefore, if prototypical or empathic emotions are evoked in spectators, it is likelier that the object lies in personal association and reminiscence than in fiction or artefact. As said, prototypical emotions will, in this case, be classified as identification. Yet, identification and empathy will probably be less intense than the task emotions of spectating.

In summary, the hypotheses following the psychological perspective can be formulated as the identification hypothesis and the emotion hypothesis. The latter consists of several parts, depending on whether you follow Tan (1996) or Konijn (1997; Hoorn & Konijn, 1999). Stating that spectators mainly experience prototypical emotions parallel to the represented character emotions on stage, the identification hypothesis is contrasted with hypotheses concerning empathy (Tan, 1994; Zillmann, 1994) or positive task emotions (Konijn, 1997) as the prevailing emotional experiences of spectators. Furthermore, hypotheses are tested that concern the objects of spectators' emotions. Tan stated that the object of spectators' emotions lies in the fiction or the artefact, whereas Konijn argued that the object may also be personal reminiscences and associations. Specifically, in the case of prototypical emotions or empathy, Konijn expected the object to lie in personal reminiscences and associations.

## METHOD

### Performances and Participants

Selected by a jury of experts, the most interesting performances of the year in The Netherlands are shown again at the Theater Festival in September. Appendix A shows the top nine performances of the 1994–1995 season that were visited by approximately 5,330 spectators. At the entrance of the theaters, visitors were randomly given one of three versions of a questionnaire (A, B, or C). They were asked to fill in the questionnaire after having seen the performance. Altogether, 757 respondents adequately completed the questionnaires (A, B, or C) at the various performances. For distributions of respondents across questionnaire versions, see Appendix A. The low response rate may be due to the length of performances (most lasted from 3 to 6 hr, sometimes without a break), the late hour, lack of fresh air and high temperatures in the theaters, fatigue with filling in questionnaires each year at every performance, and the length and difficulty of the questionnaire.

## Questionnaire

Because emotions and levels of complexity or conventionality usually vary strongly during the course of a performance, spectators were asked to answer only for a self-selected scene or fragment that, in their view, was most salient, most successful, most appealing, and most memorable. Apart from the sociological variables, all questions referred to this particular scene. Remarkably, 50% chose a scene without a central character. If a central character occurred, 60% of the characters were women. Hence, instead of *character emotions, staged emotions* would be the appropriate term. Mostly, the chosen scene was from the middle of the play.

*Sociological variables.* With reference to the sociological perspective, spectators were asked to give their age, sex, educational level, frequency of theatergoing, and whether they were active in the theater (and if so, in what way). Eversmann (1992) considered the latter an important indicator for cultural activity. In addition, spectators rated their appreciation for (different aspects of) the performance on a 10-point rating scale (Dutch school marks) ranging from 1 (*bad*) to 10 (*excellent*). Appreciation was asked for the performance as a whole but also for separate aspects: the content of the play, the decorum, the acting, and the vision of the theater makers.

*Complexity and conventionality.* Because "experts" in this line of research usually estimate the degree of complexity and conventionality of performances, the question arose whether *complex* meant "simple for the elite and difficult for others" or "difficult for the elite and incomprehensible for others." Therefore, in this study, spectators rated the degrees of complexity and conventionality as experienced by themselves. Another problem was that, in the literature at hand, complexity and conventionality as product characteristics are not always clearly distinguished from spectators' characteristics. High complexity may be relative to the level of information-processing capacity, which, in turn, may be relative to a high educational level. In addition, the level of conventionality may be determined by one's professional status (Maas et al., 1990). In the operationalization of the product characteristics, complexity and unconventionality are not always clearly distinguished. Particularly, the questionnaire used by Ganzeboom and Ranshuysen (1994) and Maas et al. (1990) was criticized by different scholars, mainly on methodological and psychometric grounds (Blok, 1995; Boter, 1997, pp. 77–94; Knulst, 1991; van den Broek, 1991). Therefore, new scales were developed, according to general psychological procedures for scale construction (Dillman, 1979; Oosterveld, 1996; van den Brink & Mellenbergh, 1998). Based on the theoretical information of Ganzeboom (1989) and Maas et al. (1990), 4 × 8 (32) statements were formulated, each followed by a 5-point rating scale, ranging from 0 (*not at all*) to 4 (*very strongly*). Each statement was supposed to reflect one of the four dimensions: complexity (e.g., "the scene was like a difficult puzzle," "contained much information," "gave new insights") or noncomplexity (e.g., "the scene had a clear meaning," "I could follow the story easily"), and unconventionality (e.g., "the portrayed situation was bizarre," "the behavior of the characters was strange") or conventionality (e.g., "this scene displayed common norms and values," "the characters behaved realistically").

*Identification.* To test the identification hypothesis from the Aristotelian paradigm, 16 prototypical emotions were included in the questionnaire (after Konijn, 1994): 8 negative (e.g., disgust, fear, anger, sadness) and 8 positive emotions (e.g., in love, pleasure, desire, tension—tension or suspense is considered a positive experience in the theater). A 5-point rating scale followed each item, ranging from 0 (*not at all*) to 4 (*very strongly*). Respondents were asked to rate the intensity of each emotion on stage (e.g., expressed by the character) and, in another section of the questionnaire, for themselves. The section of the staged emotions was disguised by questions concerning recall of the play and the selection of a particular scene.

*Emotions.* Since the emotion-psychology paradigm has a different perspective on spectators' emotions than the Aristotelian, questions on a range of emotions from different categories were also asked: based on Tan (1996), five empathic emotions (e.g., pity, involvement, affection); after Konijn (1994), seven positive task emotions (e.g., concentration, excitement, admiration) and four negative task emotions (e.g., confusion, irritation, boredom). Furthermore, the object of emotion was asked for the character's and the spectator's emotions separately. Based on Tan, five items were constructed for objects of emotion in the fiction: character or role, relationships between characters, content of the story, meaning of the event, and portrayed situation. Also, five items for objects of emotion in the artefact were constructed: stage design, text, sounds or music, special effects, and the actor's performance. The latter was added because empirical findings of Eversmann and van der Zwaal (1997, p. 26) hinted at the importance of the actor's performance for spectators' appreciation. Furthermore, five items were formulated concerning the object of the spectator's emotions in his or her personal reminiscences, associations, recognition of a person, recognition of own experiences, and recognition of oneself in the particular scene. Each item was followed by a 5-point rating scale, ranging from 0 (*not at all*) to 4 (*very strongly*).

## RESULTS

The results of statistical analyses are presented first for the sociological and then for the psychological paradigms. Each section ends with an analysis on appreciation. A significance level of $\alpha = .001$ was used for all subsequent statistical tests.

### Results on Sociological Variables

Table 1 displays the socioeconomic characteristics of respondents visiting the top nine performances at the Theater Festival 1995. According to the high-status hypothesis of the sociological perspective, the audiences of the Theater Festival should mainly consist of high-status spectators. The results do reflect a generally high-status audience, who are in their 30s, have an educational level close to academic, and are regular theatergoers. Groups of higher and lower educational levels could not be compared because the latter were hardly represented among the spectators of the Theater Festival 1995 (and because the data on education are not available for versions B or C; see the notes in Appendix A and Table 1). In addition, more than 50% of the participants were active in the theater themselves, in one way or another (amateur, professional, theater critic, theater director, etc.), pointing at their cultural activity. A positive correlation, $r(355) = .48, p < .001$, was found between being active in the theater and theatergoing. As an additional finding, the mean appreciation was lower for those who were active in the theater ($M = 7.67, SD = 1.49, n = 181$) than for those who were not ($M = 8.26, SD = 1.25, n = 168$), according to $t$ test, $t(347) = 3.93, p < .001$. Otherwise, no statistical differences were found between these groups (e.g., active vs. not active spectators did not differ in their [objects of] emotions). Among the sociographic variables (age, sex, and education), no significant or substantial ($r > .40$) correlations were found, nor were they found among the other relevant variables (e.g., appreciation,

TABLE 1
Characteristics of Spectators[a] Visiting the Top Nine Performances at the Theater Festival 1995, Amsterdam

| Variable | % (or M) | Value Label (or SD) |
|---|---|---|
| Male | 43% | |
| Female | 57% | |
| Mean age | 36 | $SD = 13.04$ |
| Education | 88% | (Equal to) university training[b] |
| Activities | 52% | Closely related to theater (amateur or professional) |
| Frequency | >50% | >6 times a year visiting theater |
| Mean frequency | 4 | Times a year visiting theater |
| Mean rating of plays | 8 | Bad 1 2 3 4 5 6 7 8 9 10 Excellent, $SD = 1.41$ |

[a]$N = 359$. [b]This result is generalized from the parallel study, with Version A of the questionnaire, reported in Eversmann and van der Zwaal (1997).

complexity, and specific emotions). For example, no significant group differences were found between women and men, age groups, or from frequency of theatergoing (Konijn, 1997).

## Results on Complexity and Conventionality

Although the scales for the (non)complexity and (un)conventionality dimensions were constructed with eight items each (see the Method section), scale analysis of the (non)complexity items showed that complexity resulted in two dimensions with four items each: Difficulty and Polyvalence. Their counterpart was Simplicity (six items). Furthermore, two relatively independent unipolar dimensions were established for Conventionality (six items) and Unconventionality (seven items).[2]

Intercorrelations between these subscales showed that the Conventionality and Simplicity subscales were more or less dependent because they showed the highest positive correlation (see Table 2). Conventionality also increased slightly when Polyvalence increased, but Simplicity was not negatively related to Polyvalence, or vice versa. As expected, Difficulty increased when Simplicity decreased and when Unconventionality increased. The relatively low to moderate intercorrelations indicate that the subscales should be considered relatively independent, except for the relation between conventional and simple.

Multivariate analysis of variance indicated that the Simplicity scale had the highest score ($M = 2.6$, $SD = .79$), followed by Polyvalence ($M = 2.00$, $SD = .88$), whereas the Difficulty scale obtained the lowest score ($M = .64$, $SD = .72$). The mean for the Conventionality scale ($M = 1.94$, $SD = .77$) was higher than that of the Unconventionality scale ($M = 1.34$, $SD = .87$): Pillai's Trace $= .72$, $F(4, 164) = 104.86$, $p < .001$. Mean ratings for the constituents of complexity and for (un)conventionality per performance are found in Appendix B. These findings are contrary to the expectation that the highest scores for Complexity and Unconventionality would occur among high-status audiences.

According to a selective stepwise multiple-regression procedure,[3] the only significant main effect found was for the Polyvalence scale in contributing to the overall appreciation, $R^2(1, 164) = .11$, $SE\ B = .116$, $\beta = .33$, $t = 4.53$, $p < .001$, two-tailed. None of the other so-called complexity or conventionality product characteristics contributed to the appreciation of these "high-brow" spectators for the performances.

---

[2]Internal consistencies (Cronbach's α, $180 < n < 185$, only Version B, see Appendix A) for the subscales of the (non)complexity items are Difficulty (four items), .67; Polyvalence (four items), .66; and, for their counterpart, Simplicity (six items), .76. Cronbach's alpha levels for the subscales of the (un)conventionality items are Conventionality (six items), .70; and Unconventionality (seven items), .78.

[3]Because variables are not uncorrelated, it is safer not to use the simple multiple-regression analysis. Furthermore, the stepwise selective-regression analysis is conservative (regarding a significant contribution to $R^2$) and parsimonious (regarding the selection of variables with the highest partial correlation with the dependent variable). The highest $R^2$ is obtained with a minimum of required variables, $p(\text{in}) = .05$, $p(\text{out}) = .10$.

TABLE 2
Intercorrelations Between Subscales for Complexity and Conventionality

|  | Difficulty | Polyvalence | Unconventionality | Simplicity |
|---|---|---|---|---|
| Polyvalence | .10 | — | — | — |
| Unconventionality | .24* | .13 | — | — |
| Simplicity | −.45** | .22* | −.03 | — |
| Conventionality | −.16 | .36** | −.10 | .59** |

*Note.* $n = 175$ (Version B, see Appendix A).
*$p < .01$. **$p < .001$ (both $p$ values are two-tailed).

## Results on Identification

Figure 1 displays the mean rated intensities of prototypical emotions on stage, including characters (dashed line), and of spectators (solid line) per item. The prototypical emotions, as noted earlier, are "the big emotions," which are central features of characters. They are supposed to underlie identification with the character. In general, the mean intensities of the character emotions on stage (as seen by the spectators) were stronger than spectators' own emotional intensities (dash > solid), except for pleasure. According to paired $t$ tests, pleasure on stage ($M = 2.46$, $SD = 1.15$) was not statistically different from spectators' pleasure ($M = 2.60$, $SD = 1.30$), $t(175) = -1.44$, $p = .15$ (Konijn, 1997). However, even if intensities of emotion do not differ, this does not necessarily imply that there is correspondence between them. Conversely, emotions that are related may not have the same intensities. Thus, correlational analyses are decisive, and these are represented on the right-hand side of Figure 1.

Because the distributions of the emotion responses are strongly skewed, a methodological problem occurred. Many emotions do not apply to either a specific character or spectator, or both, and both character and spectator received the highest score for the same emotion in only a few cases. Thus, many zeros and a few outliers caused problems for correlational analyses (Konijn & Hoorn, 1998; van den Oord & van der Ark, 1997). Therefore, a selection procedure was devised. If, for instance, the results for "in love" were analyzed, only those spectators who attributed that emotion to the character were included in the analysis. Obviously, if a particular emotion is not present on stage, a comparison between staged and spectators' emotions does not make sense.[4] Furthermore, the criterion for a significant and sufficiently strong correlation was (and should be) set to a minimum of $r = .60$ and $p < .001$ (Konijn, 1994; Konijn & Hoorn, 1998; see also Appendix C). Within these restrictions, only for eroticism can the staged ($M =$

---

[4]Because of the type of selection procedure used, the results presented in Figure 1 are on item level ($n$ varies per emotion: $118 < n < 290$) and cannot be performed on scale level. Correlations easily become significant with $n > 50$ (Guilford, 1956; Pearson & Hartley, 1956), which brings the strength of correlations into the focus of interest (see also Appendix C).

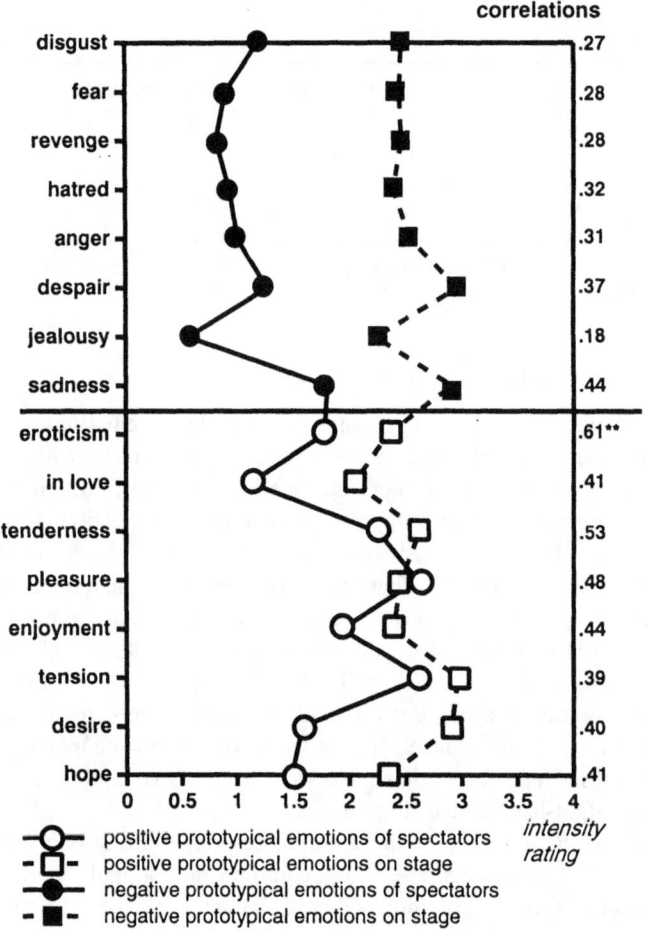

FIGURE 1  Mean intensities of prototypical emotions on stage and of spectators.

2.34, $SD = 1.06$) and spectators' ($M = 1.78$, $SD = 1.33$) emotions be considered to correspond, $r(184) = .61, p < .001$, the latter with a lesser intensity. It does not seem reasonable to consider 1 hit against 15 misses as support for the identification hypothesis. In the same vein, despite the equal intensities of pleasure in the spectator and pleasure presented on stage, they do not correspond.

## Results on Empathy and Task Emotions

Figure 2 shows the mean intensity of empathy and task emotions per item, indicating that spectators experienced empathic and positive task emotions intensively. Negative task emotions played a subordinate role. At scale level, Figure 3 shows

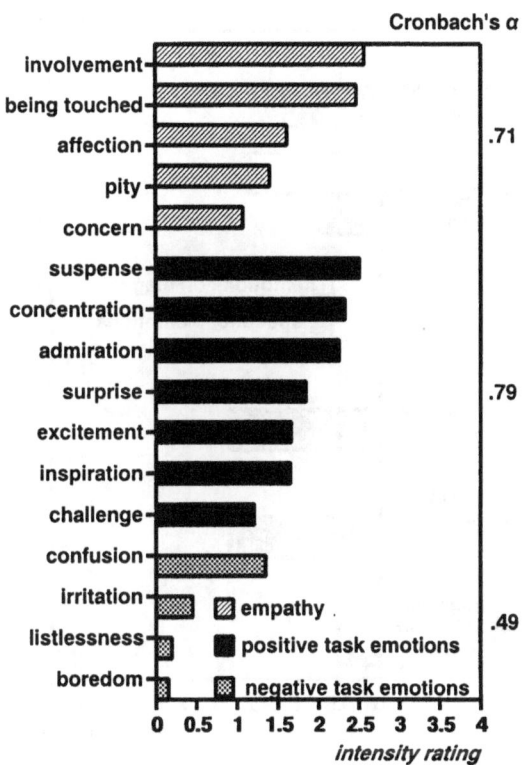

FIGURE 2   Mean intensity of empathy and task emotions per item.

that positive task emotions ($M = 1.83$, $SD = .87$) were more intense than (positive) prototypical emotions ($M = 1.20$, $SD = .84$), $t(317) = 14.61$, $p < .001$. Mean intensities of positive task emotions ($M = 1.83$, $SD = .88$) equaled empathy ($M = 1.82$, $SD = .90$), $t(328) = 0.13$, $p = .89$.

The correlation between positive task emotions and empathy was low but significant, $r(329) = .37$, $p < .001$. Empathy correlated equally with all other emotion categories, that is, with positive prototypical, $r(323) = .37$, $p < .001$, and with negative prototypical emotions, $r(337) = .39$, $p < .001$. The correlation between positive task and positive prototypical emotions also was significant and sufficient, $r(318) = .59$, $p < .001$, which seems partly to be due to the item "pleasure" in the positive prototypical scale (see the Discussion section). However, one should realize that large sample sizes easily make correlations significant.

According to stepwise regression analysis,[5] positive task emotions and empathy contributed significantly and equally to the overall appreciation, explaining

---

[5]See explanation in footnote 3.

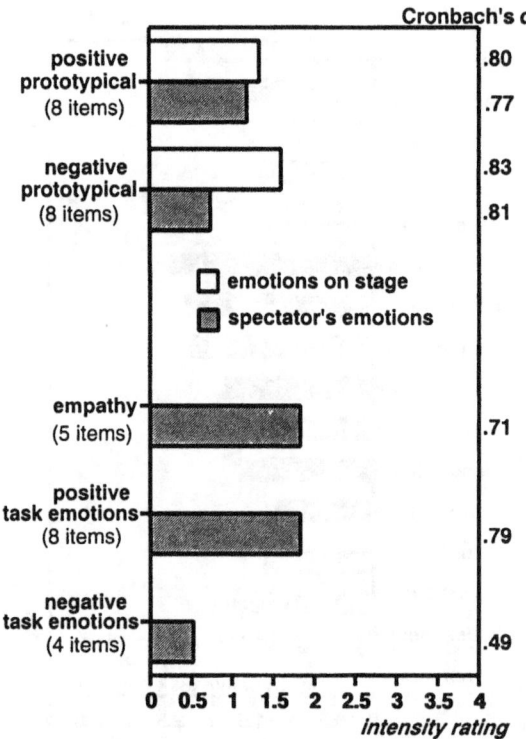

FIGURE 3  Grand mean intensity of empathy, task, and prototypical emotions at scale level.

13% of the variance, $R^2(2, 298) = .13$: for positive task, $SE\ B = .095$, $\beta = .213$, $t = 3.56$, $p < .001$, and for empathy, $SE\ B = .093$, $\beta = .210$, $t = 3.54$, $p = .001$. None of the other emotion categories contributed to the overall appreciation of the spectators of the Theater Festival 1995: for negative prototypical, $t = -.88$, $p = .38$; for positive prototypical, $t = 1.41$, $p = .16$; and for negative task emotions, $t = -2.62$, $p = .009$. These findings generally support the hypotheses derived from the psychological emotion paradigm as formulated by Tan (1994, 1996) and Konijn (1997; Hoorn & Konijn, 1999).

## Results on Object of Spectator's and Staged Emotions

Note that objects of emotion could be in the fiction (e.g., plot, character, etc.), in the artefact (e.g., decor, music, etc.), and in personal reminiscences and associations. In the scale for "object of spectator's emotion in artefact," two items did not fit according to scale analysis. One item had to be discarded, whereas the item "object of spectator's emotion [lies in the] actor's performance" was considered important enough to be used as a single item (and it had a high mean). Cronbach's

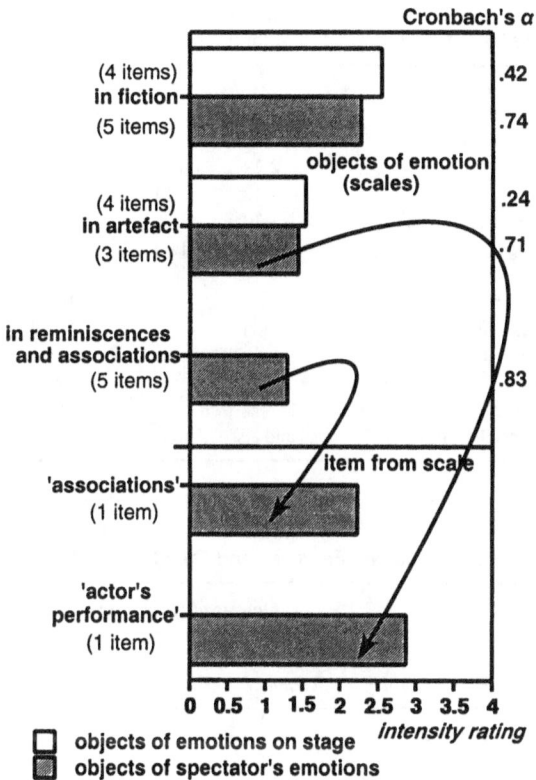

FIGURE 4  Grand mean intensity of emotion objects at scale level. Two salient items are singled out (indicated by arrows).

alphas (319 < $n$ < 329, due to missing values) for the scales concerning the objects of emotion are represented on the right-hand side of Figure 4. Figure 4 exposes the grand mean intensities for the different objects of the emotions on stage (white bars) and for those of the spectators (gray bars). The results suggest that the object of emotion was in aspects of the fiction rather than in aspects of the artefact, both on stage and for the spectator. At scale level, reminiscences and associations evoked the least intensity as object for spectators' emotions. Only when the item "own associations" was singled out from its scale was an intensity reached that was comparable with the scale "object of spectator's emotion in fiction" (Table 3). The actor's performance, analyzed as an isolated item, significantly turned out to be the strongest object of spectators' emotions.

Whether specific emotion categories are related to specific objects of emotions can be seen in Table 4.[6] Spectators' emotions were primarily related to objects in the

---

[6]No $t$ tests or correlational analyses can be performed for the objects of emotions on stage because scale reliabilities are insufficient.

TABLE 3
Means and *t* Tests for Objects of Spectators' Emotions Across Performances

|  | M | SD | t | df | p |
|---|---|---|---|---|---|
| Object of spectator's emotions: |  |  |  |  |  |
| In fiction | 2.29 | 0.95 |  |  |  |
| In artefact | 1.42 | 1.14 |  |  |  |
| In reminiscences and associations | 1.30 | 1.00 |  |  |  |
| Actor's performance | 2.87 | 1.14 |  |  |  |
| Paired *t* test |  |  |  |  |  |
| "In Fiction" × "In Artefact" |  |  | 10.84 | 305 | .00 |
| "In Reminiscences and Associations" × "In Fiction" |  |  | 14.79 | 304 | .00 |
| "In Reminiscences and Associations" × "In Artefact" |  |  | 1.11 | 314 | .27 |
| "Actor's Performance" × "In Fiction" |  |  | −9.30 | 316 | .00 |
| "Actor's Performance" × "In Artefact" |  |  | −16.85 | 328 | .00 |
| "Actor's Performance" × "In Reminiscences and Associations" |  |  | 19.81 | 323 | .00 |

TABLE 4
Correlation Matrix of Spectators' Emotions and Their Objects Across Performances

|  | Objects of Spectators' Emotions | | | |
|---|---|---|---|---|
| Spectators' Emotions | Fiction | Artefact | Reminiscences and Associations | Actor's Performance |
| Positive prototypical | .29** | .21** | .32** | .26** |
| Positive task | .38** | .30** | .29** | .36** |
| Empathy | **.54**** | .23** | .31** | .26** |
| Negative prototypical | .32** | .15* | .24** | .07 |
| Negative task | .01 | .12 | .08 | −.06 |

*Note.* *n* = 301–337 (varies because of missing data). Boldface text indicates the two highest correlations.
*$p$ < .01. **$p$ < .001 (both *p* values are two-tailed).

fiction, yet correlations were significant but not strong. Every type of emotion had weak to moderate relations with every type of object (except for negative task emotions). The strongest correlation was between empathy ($r$ = .54) and objects in fiction, partly supporting Tan's (1994) hypothesis because objects in the artefact hardly played a role for spectators' emotions. Contrary to my expectations, the emotional experiences of spectators hardly related to their personal reminiscences and associations (neither did the separate item "own associations").

Stepwise regression analysis on objects of emotion showed that objects "in fiction," "in artefact," and "actor's performance" contributed significantly to the overall appreciation, explaining 18% of the variance, $R^2(3, 281)$ = 18: for fiction, $SE\ B$ = .091, $\beta$ = .21, $t$ = 3.51, $p$ = .001; for actor's performance, $SE\ B$ = .075, $\beta$ = .20, $t$ = 3.27, $p$ = .001; and for artefact, $SE\ B$ = .067, $\beta$ = .19, $t$ = 3.51, $p$ = .001.

Because the contribution of the object of emotion "own associations" was not significant, $t = 1.56$, $p = .12$, this item did not appear to be relevant to the overall appreciation of the spectators of the Theater Festival 1995.

## DISCUSSION

### Sociological Perspective

The sociological paradigm, put forth particularly by scholars of the theory proposed by Bourdieu (1979; e.g., Ganzeboom, 1989; Maas et al., 1990), states that art increases status and that spectators choose art that is chic and in vogue. Because these researchers differ in their conceptions of high status, in this study spectators with high status were defined as highly educated, regular theatergoers, displaying much cultural activity and being in their 30s or older. The sociographic data on those attracted to the Theater Festival 1995 in Amsterdam—that is, the shows that were chic and in vogue—support this hypothesis. The finding that more than half of the spectators were closely related to the theater, as amateurs or professionals, also supports the idea of adhering to the behavior of the in-group norms. Regarding the sociographic variables age, sex, and theatergoing, no significant grouping effects were found (e.g., men's vs. women's appreciation of the performance).

As an additional finding, experience with theater probably lowers the appreciation: Those who were active in the theater appreciated performances less than those who were not active participants. On the other hand, a positive relation was found between being active in the theater and the amount of theater visits, indicating that greater experience gained by their own theatrical activities enhanced theatergoing (or vice versa). Therefore, it may be inferred, reflected by a lower appreciation rate, that more experienced theatergoers tend to be more critical than those who are less experienced. Thus, the lower appreciation rate does not necessarily reflect a lower appreciation (in the sense of liking); rather, it reflects a more critical attitude. Despite the different experience levels, there were no other differences found between these groups.

It may be argued that the participant pool was biased. Selected by a jury of experts and independent of commercial success, the Theater Festival mainly shows high-status performances that attract only a selected sample of spectators. Although the results are hard to compare with other studies, it seems that this audience at the Theater Festival 1995 had a slightly higher background than, for example, in Knulst (1989), who conducted a study at broader cultural activities, or in Maas et al. (1990), who studied a broader range of theater performances, including amateur and commercial productions. In addition, the spectators at the Theater Festival 1995 were generally higher educated, and more of them were active in the theater than in previous years (Eversmann & van der Zwaal, 1997). However, whether the spectators went to these performances to uplift their status or for reasons of prestige cannot be answered on the basis of this set of findings. To answer such a question, a measurement device should be developed for "status drives" or "prestige."

Ganzeboom (1989) and Maas et al. (1990) related the high-status hypothesis to Bourdieu's (1979) proposal that people strive for higher status by the concept of unconventionality. High-status spectators would appreciate unconventional and complex plays more than other kinds, particularly plays in an unconventional setting, that is, modern and not conservative. The authors relate complexity to Berlyne's (1970, 1974) hypothesis that a higher level of information processing increases aesthetic pleasure. Thus, high-status spectators should estimate the most interesting performances as complex and unconventional, rather than noncomplex and conventional. Based on the empirical findings, the theoretical concept complexity should be divided into two dimensions, difficulty and polyvalence, with simplicity as their counterpart. As expected, simplicity increased with an increase of conventionality, and difficulty increased when unconventionality increased (and simplicity decreased). However, not expected by the complexity hypothesis, conventionality and simplicity also increased slightly when polyvalence increased (these findings were significant but not strong). The latter finding, in particular, counters the common views on complexity and conventionality of cultural products.

Stronger counterevidence was found by Multivariate analysis of variance test, suggesting that the most interesting performances were not rated as complex (i.e., difficult) but rather as polyvalent. Simplicity had the highest score, followed by polyvalence, and difficulty was lowest. Unexpected by the complexity–conventionality hypothesis, interesting performances were not rated as unconventional but rather as conventional. Nevertheless, it may be argued that complexity (i.e., difficulty and polyvalence) and conventionality are poor discriminators among performances. Appendix B indicates that, per performance, the means for difficulty, polyvalence, and conventionality are comparable. However, the selection of performances by a jury may have raised a biased sample, as noted. Because the spectators were highly educated and were experienced theatergoers, variations in complexity (i.e., difficulty and polyvalence) and unconventionality ratings may not have occurred.

In conclusion, ideas concerning the product characteristics should be specified. Complexity should be envisioned as difficulty or polyvalence. In addition, both failed to coincide with unconventionality. High-status spectators evaluated the selected performances at the Theater Festival (1995) not as complex and unconventional. Yet, the polyvalence of the performance did contribute significantly to the overall appreciation, whereas none of the other product characteristics did.

## Psychological Perspective

According to the Aristotelian paradigm, reflected by the identification hypothesis, emotions represented by characters on stage should be paralleled by similar spectators' emotions. For identification, the focus should be on basic or prototypical emotions because they are representative for (main) characters on stage (Konijn, 1994, in press). Generally speaking, spectators rated their own emotions in this category as less intense than those performed on stage, particularly with regard to the negative prototypical emotions. Although the mean for pleasure on stage equaled the mean for spectators' pleasure, the staged emotions hardly corresponded to spectators' emotions. Only eroticism raised a significant and sufficiently strong correlation, but the intensity of spectators' erotic feelings was less than on stage. However, correspondence for 1 of 16 emotions cannot be considered convincing support for the identification hypothesis. Analyzed for separate performances, particular emotions (mainly positive ones) in a particular performance occasionally showed a significant and sufficient correlation between staged and spectators' emotions (Konijn, 1997). In addition, more than half of the spectators chose a scene without a central character, yet reported feeling intense emotions. Identification, thus, appears to be the exception rather than the rule.

Within the emotion paradigm, based on contemporary psychology, the strongest aesthetic experiences of spectators in the theater can be identified as empathy (supporting the ideas of Tan, 1994, 1996) and as positive task emotions (supporting the ideas of Konijn, 1994, 1995, in press; see also Hoorn & Konijn, 1999), which were significantly stronger than prototypical emotions. Positive task emotions and empathy were equally present. Because the correlation between positive task emotions and empathy was not strong, they can be considered distinguishable emotional experiences of spectators. With regard to the interrelations between different emotion categories for spectators, empathy is moderately and equally related with all the other emotion categories, implying that empathy is contagious with other emotions (or the other way around). Positive task and positive prototypical emotions should be considered overlapping emotion categories. Probably, this is mainly due to the emotion of pleasure, which was grouped with the prototypical emotions to test the identification hypothesis. In emotion psychology, pleasure is mentioned as one of the basic or prototypical emotions. However, pleasure also can be easily considered a task emotion (which is supported by factor analysis for spectators' emotions in Konijn, 1997), such as enjoying the acting. Furthermore, prototypical emotions turned out to be unimportant for the spectator's appreciation of the performance. In support of both Konijn (1997; Hoorn & Konijn, 1999) and Tan (1996), positive task emotions and empathy contributed significantly and equally to overall appreciation.

Concerning the question of whether particular emotions are related to a particular object, Tan (1996) expected that empathy most strongly relates to fictional objects (content). Tan also expected that spectators' emotions (undifferentiated) relate to objects concerning the artefact (form). In this article, I argue that the object may also be personal reminiscences and associations, specifically when it concerns empathy or prototypical emotions. The results show that objects of emotions in the theater are found mainly in fictional aspects, both on stage and for the spectator. According to the mean intensities, aspects concerning the artefact and personal reminiscences and associations only play a moderate role. At odds with expectation, empathy and prototypical emotions were not strongly related to personal reminiscences and associations. Perhaps clearer results will be found when a more sensitive device is developed to measure this kind of largely unconscious process. Supporting Tan, the strongest correlation was found between empathy and objects in fiction, yet not exclusively because every type of emotion had weak relations with every type of object. Thus, emotions of spectators cannot be differentiated on the basis of particular objects. Moreover, whether the objects of spectators' emotions in the fiction related to the task of understanding the fiction or "being drawn into it" cannot be distinguished here. In this respect, an additional finding is interesting: The actor's performance (as object of spectators' emotions) is significantly related to the object of spectators' emotions in the fiction, $r(317) = .45$, $p < .001$, and not with artefact, $r(329) = .07$, $p = .21$, or own associations, $r(324) = .07$, $p = .19$ (Konijn, 1997). This raises questions such as whether spectators differentiate between actor and character. Remarkably, the actor's performance turned out to be the strongest object of spectators' emotions. This is clearly not a fictional aspect but may refer to understanding the actor's play and admiring or enjoying the actor's performance. Therefore, this may count as support for the theory advanced by this study, namely that task emotions strongly regulate the aesthetic experiences of spectators in the theater.

It is interesting to note that the theater critic Esslin (1987, p. 78) already pointed out that the audience does not only come to witness events full of suspense, emotion, and interesting trials and tribulations that appear as real as possible but also to enjoy the skill with which the illusion is produced in the theater. Likewise, after the most lifelike and compelling performance, the spectator praises the acting as "splendidly natural" or that it was "just like real." Moreover, the spectator has expectations as to the correct degree of involvement of actors (and audience) in different genres of theater and acting styles: "If self-involvement at each level of role-enactment appears too little or too much for each type of theater they know, spectators may judge role-enactment as unconvincing or displeasing" (Constantinidis, 1988, p. 75). Indeed, it is likely that spectators base their choice to attend a certain performance on these expectations (e.g., concerning the reality level of portrayed emotions, the demands on a critical reflective attitude, or the expected self-disclosure). Their appreciation will probably follow accordingly. The question arises as to whether the results of this study bear not only on the theater spectator but also on viewers of cinema and television, particularly with respect to the appreciation of the actor's performance.

## SPOTLIGHT ON SPECTATORS: SUMMARIZING CONCLUSIONS

Theater performances that are in vogue are visited by high-status spectators. They generally find such a performance simple, quite conventional, and polyvalent. Only the latter contributes significantly to their overall appreciation.

While they watch a very moving scene from such a performance, identification is marginal, whereas positive task emotions (e.g., concentration on the acting) and empathy (e.g., "I feel sorry for that poor thing") are strongly represented.

It should be noted, however, that emotion words cannot be categorized easily. For instance, positive task emotions overlap with positive prototypical emotions. In addition, precise meanings of emotion words differ according to the context in which they occur. Pleasure as a character's emotion, for example, has to be distinguished from pleasure as a spectator's emotion.

Yet, task emotions and empathy are quite distinguishable and should be considered as separate and important emotion categories among audience members in the theater.

The object of spectators' emotions (positive task, empathy, etc.) is most often in the fiction (content, dramatic situation, character, etc.) rather than in the artefact (form, decor, music, etc.) or evoked by certain personal associations. However, most of all, spectators are touched by the actor's performance.

## ACKNOWLEDGMENTS

Elly A. Konijn is also an associate professor of Theater, Film, and Television Studies, Utrecht University.

This study was conducted at Utrecht University and is part of the Conditions of Production and Reception project supported by a postdoctoral grant of the Research School of Literature. It initiated a second postdoctoral study, entitled Determinants of Perceiving and Experiencing Fictional Characters, supported by The Netherlands Organization of Scientific Research Grant 301–80–79 to Elly A. Konijn and Johan F. Hoorn, and conducted at *Vrije* Universiteit, Amsterdam.

Johan F. Hoorn and Astrid Westerbeek are kindly acknowledged for their invaluable help in the later stages of this study. Ed S. H. Tan is kindly acknowledged for his clarifying comments on this article. Thanks go to Peter Eversmann, Arthur Sonnen, Hedwig van der Zwaal, Jan-Willem Kleisen, and visitors of the Theater Festival in Amsterdam 1995 for their kind cooperation regarding this project.

## REFERENCES

Abbing, H. (1986). Advies cultuurwetgeving; cultuurbeleid in historisch, beleids-analytisch en juridisch perspectief [Advice on cultural law; cultural management in historical, management-analytical and juridical perspectives]. *Sociaal en Cultureel Planbureau Cahier, 51.*

Berlyne, D. E. (1970). Novelty, complexity, and hedonic value. *Perception and Psychophysics, 8,* 279–286.

Berlyne, D. E. (1974). *Studies in the new experimental aesthetics: Steps toward an objective psychology of aesthetic appreciation.* New York: Wiley.

Blok, A. (1995). *It ain't what you do, it's why you do it.* Unpublished master's thesis, Utrecht University, Utrecht, The Netherlands.

Boter, J. (1997). Marketinginformatie uit abonnementbestanden [Marketing information from data on season-ticket holders]. In A. E. Bronner, P. Ester, A. J. Olivier, W. F. Van Raaij, M. Wedel, & B. Wierenga (Eds.), *Recente ontwikkelingen in het marktonderzoek* (pp. 77–94). Haarlem, The Netherlands: De Vrieseborch.

Bourdieu, P. (1979). *La distinction: Critique sociale du jugement* [Distinction: A critique of social judgment]. Paris: Les Editions de Minuit.

Constantinidis, S. E. (1988). Rehearsal as a subsystem: Transactional analysis and role research. *New Theatre Quarterly, 4,* 64–76.

Dijkstra, K. (1992). *Lezers in Utrecht: Een empirisch onderzoek naar verschillen in leesgedrag en factoren die hierop van invloed zijn* [Readers in Utrecht: An empirical study into differences in reading behavior and affecting factors]. Unpublished doctoral dissertation, Utrecht University, Utrecht, The Netherlands.

Dillman, D. A. (1979). *Mail and telephone surveys: The total design method.* New York: Wiley.

Ekman, P. (1982). Are there basic emotions? *Psychological Review, 99,* 550–553.

Esslin, M. (1961). *Theater of the absurd.* New York: Anchor.

Esslin, M. (1987). Actors acting actors. *Modern Drama, 30,* 72–79.

Eversmann, P. (1992). *Publieksonderzoek theaterfestival 1991* [Audience survey theater festival 1991]. Unpublished manuscript, University of Amsterdam.

Eversmann, P., & van der Zwaal, H. (1997). *Publieksonderzoek theaterfestival 1995* [Audience survey theater festival 1995]. Unpublished manuscript, University of Amsterdam.

Frijda, N. H. (1986). *The emotions: Studies in emotion and social interaction.* Cambridge, England: Cambridge University Press.

Frijda, N. H. (1988). The laws of emotion. *American Psychologist, 43,* 349–358.

Ganzeboom, H. (1989). *Cultuurdeelname in Nederland* [Cultural participation in The Netherlands]. Assen, The Netherlands: Van Gorcum.

Ganzeboom, H., & Ranshuysen, L. (1994). *Handleiding publieksonderzoek culturele instellingen* [Manual of audience research in cultural institutions]. Amsterdam: Boekman.

Greenberg, B. (1976). T.V. for children: Communicator and audience perceptions. In R. Brown (Ed.), *Children and television.* London: Collier MacMillan.

Guilford, J. P. (1956). *Fundamental statistics in psychology and education.* New York: McGraw-Hill.

Hess, U., & Kleck, R. E. (1994). The cues decoders use in attempting to differentiate emotion-elicited and deliberate emotional facial expressions. *European Journal of Social Psychology, 24,* 367–381.

Hoorn, J. F., & Konijn, E. A. (1999). *Perceiving and experiencing fictional characters: Building a model.* Manuscript in preparation, Vrije Universiteit, Amsterdam.

Knulst, W. (1989). *Van vaudeville tot video: Een empirisch–theoretische studie naar verschuivingen in het uitgaan en het gebruik van media sinds de jaren vijftig* [From vaudeville to video: An empirical–theoretical study of shifts in going out and the use of media since the fifties]. Alphen aan den Rijn, The Netherlands: Sociaal en Cultureel Planbureau.

Knulst, W. (1991). De geremde vooruitgang [The inhibited progression]. *Boekmancahier, 3,* 315–324.

Konijn, E. A. (1991). What's on between the actor and his audience? Empirical analysis of emotion processes in the theatre. In G. D. Wilson (Ed.), *Psychology and performing arts* (pp. 59–74). Lisse, The Netherlands: Swets & Zeitlinger.

Konijn, E. A. (1992). Waiting for the audience: Empirical study of actors' stage flight and performance. *Tijdschrift voor Theaterwetenschap, 31/32,* 157–183.

Konijn, E. A. (1994). *Acteurs spelen emoties, vorm geven aan emoties op het toneel—Een Psychologische Studie* [Actors acting emotions: Shaping emotions on stage—A psychological study]. Amsterdam: Boom.

Konijn, E. A. (1995). Actors and emotions: A psychological analysis. *Theater Research International, 20,* 2, 132–140.

Konijn, E. A. (1997). *Emoties van toeschouwers en personages in relatie tot produktkenmerken, toeschouwerskenmerken en waardering* [Emotions of spectators and characters in relation to prod-

uct characteristics, spectator characteristics, and appreciation]. Unpublished manuscript, Institute for Media and Re/Presentation, Utrecht University, The Netherlands.
Konijn, E. A. (in press). *Acting emotions: Shaping emotions on stage from a psychological perspective*. Amsterdam: Amsterdam University Press.
Konijn, E. A., & Hoorn, J. F. (1998, September). *Zero's and outliers: Significant correlations may not reflect real relations*. Paper presented at the biannual meeting of the International Association for Empirical Aesthetics (XVth Congress of IAEA), Rome, Italy.
Konijn, E. A., & Westerbeek, A. (1997). *Acteren en emoties* [Acting and emotions]. Amsterdam: Boom.
Kreitler, H., & Kreitler, S. (1972). *Psychology of the arts*. Durham, NC: Duke University Press.
Laffont, R. (1960). *Dictionnaire des personnages, de tous les temps et de tous les pays* [Dictionary of characters, of all times and all places]. Paris: S.E.D.E. et V. Bompiani.
Maas, I., Verhoeff, R., & Ganzeboom, H. (1990). *Podiumkunsten en publiek* [Performing arts and audience]. Rijswijk, The Netherlands: Ministerie van W. V. C.
McGuire, W. J. (1974). Psychological motives and communication gratification. In J. G. Blumler & E. Katz (Eds.), *The uses of mass communications. Current perspectives on gratifications research* (pp. 167–196). Beverly Hills, CA: Sage.
Mesquita, B., Gomes de. (1993). *Cultural variations in emotions: A comparative study of Dutch, Suriname, and Turkish People in The Netherlands*. Unpublished doctoral dissertation, University of Amsterdam.
Oosterveld, P. (1996). *Questionnaire design methods*. Nijmegen, The Netherlands: Berkhout.
Pearson, E. S., & Hartley, H. O. (1956). *Biometrika tables for statisticians (I)*. Cambridge, England: Cambridge University Press.
Polti, G. (1990). *The thirty-six dramatic situations*. Boston: The Writer.
Schälzky, H. (1980). *Empirisch–quantitative methoden in der theaterwissenschaft* [Empirical and quantitative methods in theater studies]. München, Germany: Kommissionsverlag J. Kitzinger (Münchener Universitätsschriften, Philosophische Fakultät).
Schmitz, H., & Vorderer, P. (1998, August). *Experiencing a fictional world—The connection between viewers' involvement, personality, and mood*. Poster session presented at the sixth biannual conference of the International Society for the Empirical Study of Literature, IGEL. Utrecht, The Netherlands.
Schoenmakers, H. (1986). The pleasure of sorrow—Die Freude am Kummer. *Tijdschrift voor Theaterwetenschap, 16/17*, 117–150.
Schoenmakers, H. (1988). To be, wanting to be, forced to be: Identification processes in theatrical situations. *Tijdschrift voor Theaterwetenschap, 24/25*, 138–163.
Schoenmakers, H. (1990). The spectator in the leading role. In W. Sauter (Ed.), *Nordic theatre studies: New directions in theatre reseach* (pp. 93–106). Stockholm, Sweden: Munksgaard.
Schoenmakers, H. (1992). Aesthetic emotions and aestheticised emotions in theatrical situations. *Tijdschrift voor Theaterwetenschap, 31/32*, 39–59.
Schram, D. (1985). *Norm en normdoorbreking* [Norm and norm transgression]. Amsterdam: Vrije Universiteit.
Scitovsky, T. (1976). *The joyless economy*. New York: Oxford University Press.
Shields, S. A. (1984). Distinguishing between emotion and non-emotion: Judgments about experience. *Motivation and Emotion, 8*, 355–369.
Tan, E. S. H. (1994). Film-affect as induced witness emotion. *Poetics, 23*, 7–32.
Tan, E. S. H. (1996). *Emotion and the narrative structure of film*. Mahwah, NJ: Lawrence Erlbaum Associates, Inc.
van den Brink, W. P., & Mellenbergh, G. J. (1998). *Testleer en testconstructie* [Test theory and test construction]. Amsterdam: Boom.
van den Broek, A. (1991). Twee stappen vooruit en één misstap [Two steps ahead and one step wrong]. *Boekmancahier, 3*, 325–330.

van den Oord, E. J. C. G., & van der Ark, L. A. (1997). A note on the use of the Tobit approach for test scores with floor or ceiling effects. *British Journal of Mathematical and Statistical Psychology, 50,* 351–364.

van Trijp, J. C. M. (1997). Variatie-zoekend keuzegedrag van consumenten [Variety-seeking behavior of consumers]. In A. E. Bronner, P. Ester, A. J. Olivier, W. F. Van Raaij, M. Wedel, & B. Wierenga (Eds.), *Recente ontwikkelingen in het marktonderzoek* (pp. 191–209). Haarlem, The Netherlands: De Vrieseborch.

van Vliet, H. (1991). *De schone schijn: Een analyse van psychologische processen in de beleving van fictionaliteit en werkelijkheid bij theatrale produkten* [Attractive appearances: An analysis of psychological processes in the experience of fiction and reality in theatrical products]. Unpublished doctoral dissertation, Utrecht, The Netherlands.

Westerbeek, A. (1995). *Buiten spel, (non-)identificatie en steracteurs—Een theoretisch en empirisch onderzoek* [Off-side. (Non)identification and star-actors—A theoretical and empirical study]. Unpublished master's thesis, Utrecht University, Utrecht, The Netherlands.

Wildschut, L. (1995). *Bewegen en bewogen: Theoretisch en empirisch onderzoek naar de beleving van een dansvoorstelling bij kinderen* [Moving and being moved: Theoretical and empirical study into childrens' experiences at a dance performance]. Unpublished master's thesis, Utrecht University, Utrecht, The Netherlands.

Zillmann, D. (1991). Empathy: Affect from bearing witness to the emotions of others. In J. Bryant & D. Zillmann (Eds.), *Responding to the screen: Reception and reaction processes* (pp. 135–167). Mahwah, NJ: Lawrence Erlbaum Associates, Inc.

Zillmann, D. (1994). Mechanisms of emotional involvement with drama. *Poetics, 23,* 33–51.

## APPENDIX A
Performances at the Theater Festival 1995, Amsterdam, and the Number of Responses

| Performances | Response to Questionnaire | | |
|---|---|---|---|
| | Version B[a] | Version C[a] | Total[b] |
| *Angels in America* | 23 | 15 | 38 |
| *Goldberg Variaties* [Goldberg Variations] | 18 | 15 | 33 |
| *Onder Controle* [Under Control] | 39 | 40 | 79 |
| *Moeder en Kind* [Mother and Child] | 16 | 21 | 37 |
| *Rijkemanshuis* [Stately Mansion] | 32 | 28 | 60 |
| *Who's Afraid of Virginia Woolf?* | 33 | 33 | 66 |
| *Lulu* | 5 | — | 5[c] |
| *Klaagliederen* [Jeremy] | 18 | 13 | 31 |
| *Kopnaad* | 5 | 5 | 10[c] |
| Total | 189 | 170 | 359 |

*Note.* To reduce the length of the questionnaire, three parallel versions—A, B, and C—were made. Version A is reported in Eversmann and van der Zwaal (1997) and Versions B and C are reported in this article. Versions B and C shared items on character emotions (staged emotions), emotional impact, object of emotion, appreciation, and spectator characteristics. Version B uniquely contained items on complexity and conventionality (product characteristics). Version C uniquely contained items on acting quality (not presented in this article). The characteristics of the spectators reported in Table 1 were comparable between Versions B and C of the questionnaire. Thus, groups were pooled for the general analyses.

[a]Number of completed questionnaires. [b]Total number of completed questionnaires. [c]Too few responses for separate analyses.

## APPENDIX B
### Mean Ratings on Subscales for Complexity and Conventionality per Performance

| Performances and Scales | M | SD | Minimum[a] | Maximum[a] | n |
|---|---|---|---|---|---|
| *Angels in America* | | | | | |
|   Difficulty | 0.43 | 0.44 | 0.00 | 1.25 | 23 |
|   Polyvalence | 2.01 | 0.74 | 0.25 | 3.50 | 23 |
|   Simplicity | 2.62 | 0.45 | 1.50 | 3.33 | 23 |
|   Unconventionality | 1.13 | 0.63 | 0.29 | 2.71 | 22 |
|   Conventionality | 2.08 | 0.57 | 1.00 | 3.33 | 23 |
| *Goldberg Variaties* [Goldberg Variations] | | | | | |
|   Difficulty | 0.64 | 0.54 | 0.00 | 2.00 | 18 |
|   Polyvalence | 2.06 | 0.92 | 0.25 | 3.25 | 18 |
|   Simplicity | 2.68 | 0.77 | 0.50 | 3.83 | 18 |
|   Unconventionality | 0.79 | 0.60 | 0.00 | 2.14 | 18 |
|   Conventionality | 1.61 | 0.60 | 0.67 | 2.67 | 18 |
| *Onder Controle* [Under Control] | | | | | |
|   Difficulty | 0.69 | 0.77 | 0.00 | 4.00 | 38 |
|   Polyvalence | 1.99 | 0.93 | 0.00 | 3.75 | 37 |
|   Simplicity | 2.65 | 0.88 | 0.00 | 4.00 | 39 |
|   Unconventionality | 1.93 | 0.97 | 0.14 | 3.43 | 37 |
|   Conventionality | 2.05 | 0.87 | 0.00 | 3.67 | 39 |
| *Moeder en Kind* [Mother and Child] | | | | | |
|   Difficulty | 0.45 | 0.70 | 0.00 | 2.25 | 15 |
|   Polyvalence | 2.15 | 0.77 | 0.75 | 3.50 | 15 |
|   Simplicity | 2.57 | 1.02 | 0.33 | 3.83 | 14 |
|   Unconventionality | 1.99 | 1.08 | 0.00 | 3.86 | 15 |
|   Conventionality | 2.06 | 0.90 | 0.33 | 3.50 | 13 |
| *Rijkemanshuis* [Stately Mansion] | | | | | |
|   Difficulty | 0.75 | 0.71 | 0.00 | 2.75 | 30 |
|   Polyvalence | 2.32 | 0.86 | 0.00 | 3.75 | 29 |
|   Simplicity | 2.68 | 0.73 | 1.17 | 4.00 | 28 |
|   Unconventionality | 1.30 | 0.81 | 0.14 | 3.00 | 29 |
|   Conventionality | 2.13 | 0.79 | 0.67 | 3.83 | 29 |
| *Who's Afraid of Virginia Woolf?* | | | | | |
|   Difficulty | 0.44 | 0.61 | 0.00 | 2.00 | 33 |
|   Polyvalence | 1.95 | 0.76 | 0.50 | 3.25 | 33 |
|   Simplicity | 2.65 | 0.73 | 0.50 | 4.00 | 33 |
|   Unconventionality | 1.14 | 0.77 | 0.00 | 2.71 | 32 |
|   Conventionality | 1.93 | 0.68 | 0.67 | 3.17 | 33 |
| *Klaagliederen* [Jeremy] | | | | | |
|   Difficulty | 1.35 | 0.90 | 0.00 | 2.75 | 18 |
|   Polyvalence | 1.85 | 1.00 | 1.00 | 4.00 | 18 |
|   Simplicity | 1.93 | 0.78 | 0.50 | 3.17 | 16 |
|   Unconventionality | 1.08 | 0.75 | 0.00 | 3.00 | 17 |
|   Conventionality | 1.49 | 0.81 | 0.50 | 3.33 | 15 |

*Note.* The higher the score, the closer the product characteristic (e.g., difficult) fits the specific performance in the eyes of the spectator.

[a]Minimum score is 0, and maximum score is 4.

For Product Safety Concerns and Information please contact our EU
representative GPSR@taylorandfrancis.com
Taylor & Francis Verlag GmbH, Kaufingerstraße 24, 80331 München, Germany

www.ingramcontent.com/pod-product-compliance
Lightning Source LLC
Chambersburg PA
CBHW081423230426
43668CB00016B/2331